I0530848

Greek Mythology: Gods of Mount Olympus

Greek Mythology Series
by Michael J Defosse

Greek Mythology: Gods of Mount Olympus
Myths, Powers, and Legends That Shaped Ancient Greece

Coming Soon

Greek Mythology: Kingdom of Hades
Underworld Myths, Chthonic Gods, and the Secrets of the Dead

Greek Mythology: Dominion of Poseidon
Myths of Sea Gods, Ocean Monsters, and Ancient Legends of the Deep

Greek Mythology: Rise and Fall of the Titans
Primordial Gods, Titan Myths, and the Battle for the Cosmos

Greek Mythology: Illustrated Companion Guide
Gods, Heroes, Symbols, and Creatures of Ancient Greece

Step into the Realm of Gods, Beasts, and Legends — Where Myth Breathes Eternal

Receive future book updates and news:
info@mythologypublishing.com

GREEK MYTHOLOGY: GODS OF MOUNT OLYMPUS

MYTHS, POWERS, AND LEGENDS THAT SHAPED ANCIENT GREECE

BY MICHAEL J DEFOSSE

Mythology Publishing

GREEK MYTHOLOGY: GODS OF MOUNT OLYMPUS

Copyright © 2025 Michael J. Defosse
Publishing rights granted to Mythology Publishing LLC

This book incorporates the use of artificial intelligence (AI) tools in the creation and editing of certain elements, including illustrations and cover design. AI technology was used as a creative aid to enhance the storytelling and visual presentation, under the careful guidance and oversight of the author to ensure accuracy, authenticity, and quality. All content has been reviewed, curated, and refined by the author to maintain historical accuracy, thematic consistency, and a captivating reader experience. The collaboration between human creativity and AI innovation is intended to deliver a fresh and engaging perspective on the timeless tales of Greek mythology.

All rights reserved. No part of this publication may be reproduced, stored in a retrieval system, or transmitted in any form or by any means, electronic, mechanical, photocopying, recording, scanning, or otherwise, except as permitted under Section 107 or 108 of the 1976 United States Copyright Act without the prior written permission of the author.

For inquiries, contact Mythology Publishing at:
info@mythologypublishing.com

ISBN: 979-8-9997003-0-8 (Paperback)
ISBN: 979-8-9997003-1-5 (Hardcover)

Library of Congress Control Number: 2025916931

First Edition
10 9 8 7 6 5 4 3 2 1

Printed in the United States of America
Published in New York, NY

DEDICATION

To the dreamers, the adventurers, and the seekers of
hidden worlds—
To those who find magic in the whispered myths of old
and wonder in the shadows of ancient folklore—
To every reader who has ever wandered through
enchanted forests, sailed uncharted seas, or stood at the
gates of realms beyond—

This book is dedicated to you.

May these tales ignite your imagination, stir your spirit, and
remind you that legends never truly fade. They continue to
live in the hearts of those who believe.

Thank you for journeying with me into the timeless world
of myths and stories.

Scrolls of Olympus

PREFACE

To the ancient Greeks, the divine was not distant. It breathed in thunder, stirred beneath the sea, and watched from the mountaintop veiled in cloud. The world was alive with gods—flawed, magnificent, eternal—and none stood higher than the twelve who ruled from Olympus.

Greek Mythology: Gods of Mount Olympus is an invitation to ascend that sacred peak. Before temples were raised in their honor and poets carved their names into epic verse, these deities shaped the hearts and hopes of a civilization. They governed the skies, the seas, the harvest, and the hearth. Their myths were more than tales—they were mirrors of mortal yearning and celestial law.

This book does not merely recount the stories of the Olympians—it seeks to rekindle their presence, to walk once more among gods who laugh, rage, love, and judge with immortal fire. Whether you come as a student, seeker, or storyteller, may you find in these pages the grandeur, mystery, and enduring power of the gods who shaped the Western imagination.

The journey begins on Olympus. From there, the divine unfolds.

INTRODUCTION

Gods of Mount Olympus

B efore ink touched parchment and epic verse etched gods into eternity, the tales of the gods were passed from lips to firelight, whispered beneath the open sky and etched into the soul of a people. These were not mere amusements, but sacred revelations—stories woven to explain the thunder in the clouds, the fury of the sea, the fickleness of fate, and the greatness and grief within every mortal heart. At the center of this mythic tapestry rose Mount Olympus, a hallowed summit where the immortal met the mortal, and from its heights, the Olympian gods cast their will upon the world below.

> *"Begin, O Muse, and tell of the gods who dwell on Olympus,*
> *who give both blessings and misfortunes to mortals,*
> *for such is their will and unchanging fate."*
> — *Homeric Hymn to the Gods*

Greek mythology stands as a pillar of Western thought—its echoes resounding through literature, art, and the endless search for truth. In these tales of defiance and devotion, of passion and punishment, the ancients preserved their worldview: a vision shaped by wonder and warning, by hope and celestial justice. These myths are not relics of the past; they are mirrors of the soul, reflecting the eternal questions of who we are, why we suffer, and what destiny awaits.

This book is your invitation into that mythic realm. Here, you will walk among the immortals, from Zeus, the storm-crowned ruler of the heavens, to Dionysus, the reveler who breaks all boundaries. Through their myths and mysteries, you will discover how the Olympians shaped not only the world of ancient Greece, but the very language of power, nature, and human desire. The journey begins now—into a world where gods ruled, mortals dared, and legends were born to live forever.

ORIGIN OF GREEK MYTH

Greek mythology emerges as a radiant tapestry of numinous memory, woven from the golden threads of oral tradition and bound by the echoes of a world still cloaked in mystery. These ancient tales sprang forth when the earth was untamed and the skies alive with portents—when a thunderclap was the voice of a god and the sea's fury the wrath of unseen powers. To the people of early Greece, the gods were not distant celestial concepts, but living forces—volatile, commanding, and ever-present in the rhythms of life and death, harvest and storm, war and love.

Passed from tongue to tongue, shaped by poet and priest, the myths deepened with every telling. The verses of Homer's *Iliad* and *Odyssey*, the cosmic origins of Hesiod's *Theogony*, and countless lost hymns and tragedies gave structure to the divine. Through these works, the pantheon took shape—not as flawless ideals, but as mighty beings bearing the full spectrum of human emotion: pride and desire, vengeance and longing, rivalry and redemption—each elevated by their immortal might.

At the heart of these sacred tales stood Mount Olympus, veiled in cloud and crowned with glory. This celestial throne was no mere mountain—it was the axis of heavenly law, the meeting place between the eternal and the ephemeral. There, the Olympians dined on ambrosia and sipped nectar, their laughter shaking the heavens, their judgments shaping the world below. Olympus was both real and imagined, a realm of god-forged order where mortal dreams rose like smoke to the halls of the undying.

OLYMPIANS TAKE SHAPE

Mount Olympus, the sacred throne of the immortals, rose not only as the highest peak in Greece but as the spiritual pinnacle of divine rule. Crowned with shifting clouds and steeped in myth, it stood as both a literal and symbolic summit—a celestial citadel where the gods convened in splendor. At its zenith, Zeus presided over a court of immortals, each deity sovereign of a realm, a force of nature personified, a myth brought to life.

Yet the Olympians were never paragons of perfection. They clashed, conspired, and entangled themselves in mortal affairs with awe-inspiring power and perilous consequence. But in their flaws, they revealed their brilliance—for it was not purity that defined them, but intensity. Their passions surged like rivers of fire: Hera's relentless love, Ares's consuming fury, Athena's piercing intellect, Hermes' boundless cunning. In these mythic dramas, the Greeks uncovered mirrors of themselves—fables rich with meaning, offering both guidance and warning on the path of life.

More than celestial rulers, the Olympian gods embodied the ideals of a thriving civilization. Zeus, with his thunder and decrees, symbolized justice and the might of kingship. Athena, ever-strategic and wise, reflected the disciplined mind and valor needed to endure a world of war and uncertainty. Apollo, radiant god of prophecy and song, inspired the pursuit of beauty, knowledge, and order. Each deity stood as a guardian of a truth, a living emblem of what the Greeks valued most—offering protection, inspiration, and an Olympian measure against which mortals might rise.

INSIDE THIS BOOK

Within these pages lies a journey through the mythic heart of ancient Greece—a voyage into the world of the Olympian gods and the stories that shaped a civilization. This book unveils the primordial intrigues of the immortals: their rivalries and romances, their thunderous quarrels and whispered alliances, and the way their actions echoed across the mortal realm, sculpting the beliefs and values of an entire culture.

You will see how the gods were honored in grand temples and sacred festivals—how Zeus's thunderous reign inspired the Olympic Games, and how devotion was expressed in ritual, offering, and myth. The sacred bonds between gods and mortals, between earth and sky, unfold in tales of power and passion, of wisdom and wrath. These legends illuminate eternal themes— justice, loyalty, ambition, and the fragile balance between hubris and humility.

More than myth, this exploration is a portal into the soul of an ancient people. Through the lens of art, ritual, and philosophy, readers will come to understand how mythology was not mere story but a living force—a sacred mirror reflecting the ideals, fears, and aspirations of Greece. In doing so, they will discover how these timeless narratives continue to shape the imagination and spirit of Western civilization.

WHAT TO EXPECT

This book unfolds as a sacred procession through the pantheon of Mount Olympus, with each chapter devoted to a single deity— an immortal whose stories, powers, and symbols shaped the ancient world. We begin with Zeus, sovereign of thunder and law, and ascend through the myths of Hera, Poseidon, Demeter, Athena, Apollo, Artemis, Ares, Aphrodite, Hephaestus, Hermes, Hestia, and Dionysus—each a force of nature, each a pillar of mythic identity.

Within every chapter, distinct sections guide us through the many faces of the god or goddess—revealing their most celebrated myths, tracing the origins of their celestial might, and exploring the rituals, temples, and iconography that kept their presence alive in the hearts of mortals. These sacred portraits are woven together with revelations on the deeper themes of Greek mythology: its echoes in philosophy, its imprint on politics and art, and its enduring call to wonder.

By the book's end, you will not only know the Olympian gods— you will have walked in their world, seen with mythic eyes, and felt the ancient pulse that still beats beneath our stories. This is more than a study of the divine; it is an invitation to rediscover the timeless power of mythology to illuminate, challenge, and unite us across the vast river of time.

ETERNAL FLAME OF MYTH

To understand the Olympian gods, one must first enter the world that gave rise to their legends—a world where myth and reality moved as one. Ancient Greece was a land of radiant contradiction: jagged mountains and tranquil temples, fierce rivalries and shared divinities. The gods were not distant abstractions; they were living forces, invoked in oaths and omens, present in battle cries, harvest prayers, and household shrines.

Religion was not confined to ritual—it flowed through every facet of Greek life. The myths reflected and reinforced the ideals of the people: heroism, justice, wisdom, and the struggle to find order in chaos. Artists gave the gods form in marble and bronze; poets gave them voice in epic verse; philosophers, even as they questioned, could not escape the mythic lens through which Greece viewed the cosmos.

And still, these gods endure.

The Olympians live on across centuries because they embody something universal—desire, vengeance, love, defiance, and awe. In their flawed grandeur, we see ourselves magnified. Their stories are not relics; they are reflections—living flames that ignite the imagination. They walk beside us in modern tales, on screen and stage, in books and belief. Mythology remains a bridge between mortal and immortal, calling each generation to rediscover what it means to dream, to struggle, and to seek meaning beneath the stars.

WHY THESE MYTHS ENDURE

The Olympian myths endure not because they are old, but because they are true in a deeper sense—true to the eternal questions of the human soul. We return to them not for answers, but for insight, for wonder, for the sense that something greater walks beside us in the storm, the silence, and the stars.

To hear these stories is to remember that we are part of something vast—where the celestial touches the mortal, and every heart echoes with the voice of a god.

CHAPTER 1

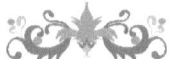

MOUNT OLYMPUS

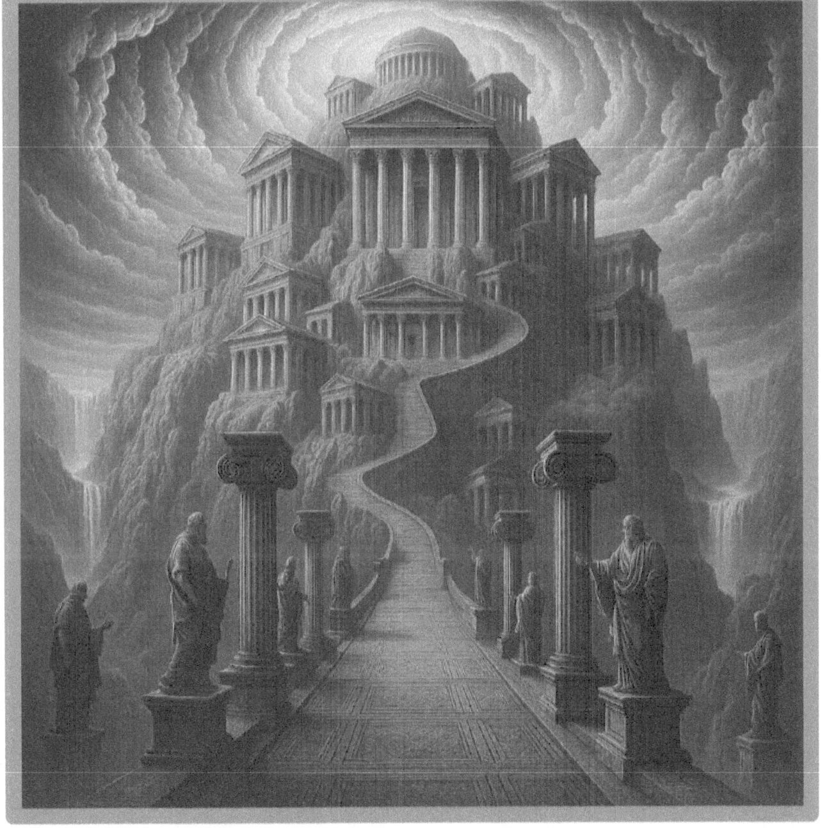

Home of the Gods

The legend of Mount Olympus unfolds as a tapestry of ethereal beginnings—where the breath of the gods stirs the clouds, and the pulse of myth beats against the sky. Crowned in mist and cloaked in mystery, this sacred peak was no ordinary mountain. Rising as the imagined threshold between earth and eternity, the mountain of the gods became a summit where storms were not accidents of nature but the language of power. Its stories shimmer with celestial wonder, echoing in the footsteps of gods and mortals bold enough to seek its heights. To trace the origin, radiant grandeur, and the rare, fateful moments when mortals entered its exalted halls, is to glimpse the sacred heartbeat of Greek mythology itself—a summit where earth touches the eternal.

> *"Olympus, where the gods dwell forever in bliss,*
> *untroubled by wind or rain or snow,*
> *and a pure air is ever spread around them,*
> *and the white radiance shines all over."*
> — *Homer, The Odyssey*

The Heavenly Mountain

In the dawn of all things, when chaos veiled the cosmos and earth lay shapeless and unformed, Mount Olympus began its ascent into myth. To the ancient Greeks, it was far more than stone and sky—it was the sacred summit where the mortal and the divine converged. Rising high above the world of men, its lofty peaks vanished into a mantle of clouds, veiling the celestial stronghold of the gods from human gaze. Olympus stood as the eternal throne of the Olympians—a symbol of god-forged rule, of power woven into the very fabric of myth and memory.

The origins of Olympus were forged in the crucible of cosmic upheaval. From the storm of the primordial age and the cataclysmic war between Titans and Olympians, Zeus and his siblings emerged triumphant, casting down the old order. To seal their dominion, they claimed the highest mountain in all of Greece—not merely as a dwelling, but as a heavenly citadel. Unlike mortal peaks, Olympus existed both in the realm of earth and beyond it: an ever-blooming paradise untouched by death or decay, where the gods lived in radiant, unending splendor.

Its soaring heights marked the boundary between heaven and earth, a reminder of the gods' dominion and the fragile thread of fate beneath which mortals toiled. Yet Olympus was not beyond reach. Though rare and perilous, moments came when mortals glimpsed its wonders or stood within its halls. Such encounters, etched in legend, revealed Olympus not only as a seat of order and might, but as the Greeks' highest ideal—a realm of harmony, immortality, and the eternal presence of the Olympians.

Forged in War, Crowned in Glory

The sacred tale of Mount Olympus is bound to the ascension of the gods and the forging of mythic order. After Zeus led his siblings to triumph in the Titanomachy—the great war that shattered the old dominion—he sought a throne worthy of their newfound power. In the whispers of myth, Olympus rose from the vanquished remains of the Titans, its jagged slopes and skyward peaks a monument to victory. Some legends speak of Gaia herself, the primordial mother, shaping the mountain as a sanctuary for her divine lineage—a cradle for gods amid the heavens.

But Olympus was no mere mountain. It was an eternal realm, unmarked by time or decay, where seasons did not turn and the sorrows of mortality held no sway. There, nectar flowed and ambrosia glowed with golden light—gifts that nourished immortals and sustained their undying might. Along its gleaming heights stood the celestial dwellings of the gods, forged by Hephaestus in fire and craft, each a palace of radiant splendor. At the summit, upon a throne of incomparable brilliance, Zeus reigned—his presence a beacon of god-forged authority and the storm-born force of law.

Mount Olympus became the stage upon which the destiny of the world was shaped. Within its halls, the gods gathered to council and contend, their quarrels echoing through the fabric of mortal fate. It was beneath this sacred firmament that Paris of Troy made his fateful choice, unleashing the winds of war that would consume an age. Here, celestial banquets sealed pacts and alliances, even as rivalries simmered beneath golden laughter.

Yet Olympus transcended the tales spun within it. It stood as a symbol of permanence, a citadel of light unmarred by the world's turbulence. As mortals labored beneath shifting skies and passing seasons, Olympus remained ever resplendent, its serenity untouched. This ethereal stillness mirrored the gods' eternal watch, their high dominion a reminder that while the mortal world churned in chaos, above it all stood an order eternal, sacred, and supreme.

When Mortals Reached Olympus

Though Mount Olympus crowned the heavens as a realm of divine purity, its gates were not sealed forever against mortal tread. In the scrolls of Greek mythology lie rare and radiant tales—

moments when mortals ascended the sacred mountain and stood beneath the gaze of the gods. Such encounters shimmered with awe and peril alike, for though the immortals could bestow glory and favor, their wrath struck with the swiftness of thunder.

Among the boldest was Bellerophon, the slayer of the Chimera and master of the winged steed Pegasus. Drunk on victory and pride, he sought not glory in battle but divinity itself. Soaring toward Olympus, he dared to claim a place among the gods. But the heavens do not yield to arrogance. Zeus, displeased by the mortal's presumption, loosed a gadfly upon Pegasus, casting Bellerophon from the skies. Though he lived, he wandered the earth in ruin—his failed ascent etched into legend as a solemn warning: mortal feet must not tread where hubris seeks to fly.

Yet not all who reached Olympus fell. Ganymede, prince of Troy, was chosen—not by ambition, but by ethereal beauty. Zeus, beholding the youth from his golden throne, descended in the form of an eagle and bore him aloft to the immortal heights. There, Ganymede was granted eternal youth and honored as cupbearer to the gods. His tale became a symbol of transcendence, where the mortal soul—favored by the divine—was lifted into eternity.

Others came by trial and devotion. Psyche, a mortal woman whose love for Eros defied even the will of the gods, endured tasks of impossible cruelty set by jealous Aphrodite. Her perseverance moved the heart of Olympus. In a final act of grace, Zeus summoned her to the mountain's summit and gifted her immortality, that she might dwell forever with her beloved. Her ascent, unlike Bellerophon's fall, was a reward—not for pride, but for fidelity, courage, and heart.

These mythic ascents were woven with more than spectacle; they embodied truths the Greeks held sacred. They revealed the rift between the mortal and immortals, and the rare bridges that might span it—heroism, beauty, unwavering devotion, or the whim of heavenly favor. Yet always they echoed the same truth: Olympus was not earned by force, but granted by grace.

In these sacred stories, the Greeks saw themselves reflected—ambitious, flawed, and yearning for the eternal. Mount Olympus, though high above the world, remained deeply entwined with it. It stood as both a summit and a symbol—a place where gods ruled, and where mortals dreamed of more. In its myths, Olympus became the eternal stage of divine justice and mortal destiny, where the heavens touched the hearts of humankind.

DOMINION OF THE SACRED PEAK

The powers of Mount Olympus echoed the god-forged authority and sacred symbolism that crowned it the ultimate refuge of the gods. Chosen as their celestial seat, Olympus embodied both physical majesty and spiritual dominion. Its radiant halls, mythic gates, and golden palaces reflected the Olympians' supremacy and their eternal rule. More than a mountain, it stood as a living testament to their command over the cosmos and their bond to the world below—its enduring presence shaping the myths, reverence, and cultural soul of ancient Greece.

"Far above all the heavens and the earth,
the gods sat on high Olympus,
where all their pleasures lay and none of their cares."
— Homer, The Iliad

Sanctuary of the Immortals

Long before Mount Olympus rose as the sanctified throne of the immortals, it stood as the loftiest peak in Greece—remote, veiled in mist, and steeped in silent majesty. In the wake of their triumph over the Titans, the Olympian gods sought a dwelling worthy of their dominion. Olympus, exalted in height and purity, was chosen not merely for its grandeur, but for its symbolic detachment from the sorrows and frailties of the mortal world. To the ancient Greeks, it was the summit of sanctity—a place unblemished by human toil.

Claiming Olympus was both a proclamation of power and a covenant of unity. With the old order buried in the abyss of Tartarus, the gods ascended not just in rank, but in realm. They turned their gaze from the depths to the heavens, enthroning themselves above the lands they now ruled. The mountain, ever-watchful across the Greek horizon, became the perfect bastion—a beacon of mythic presence, rising above the chaos they had quelled.

Yet Olympus offered more than elevation. In the sacred tales, it transcended all mortal geography. It became a liminal realm, suspended between earth and sky, where time held no dominion and death dared not tread. No scars marred its slopes, no ruin touched its soil. Here, the gods dwelled in eternal vitality, their splendor undimmed. Olympus, thus, was transformed from stone to symbol—an everlasting haven, radiant and serene, fit for those who ruled both fate and firmament.

Mythical Gates and Palaces

The splendor of Mount Olympus rose not only in height, but in divine craftsmanship—its gates, halls, and sacred precincts fashioned by immortal hands. At its threshold stood the radiant Gates of Olympus, aglow with golden light, warding the realm against all unworthy of its sanctity. These celestial portals were guarded by the Horae, goddesses of the seasons, who governed the eternal rhythms of time and nature. Through their vigilant grace, Olympus remained untouched by disorder, preserved in an everlasting state of cosmic harmony.

Beyond these hallowed gates stretched the fabled palaces of the gods—wonders wrought by Hephaestus, master of flame and forge. With celestial fire and ethereal artistry, he shaped dwellings that echoed the very essence of their inhabitants. Apollo's palace shimmered like the rising sun, steeped in radiance and song. Athena's halls bore the sigils of wisdom, gleaming with the symbols of war and insight. Poseidon's chambers murmured with the ceaseless voice of the sea, their marble walls alive with the swell and surge of tide.

At Olympus's summit towered the palace of Zeus—sovereign among gods, ruler of storm and sky. There, upon a throne of gold veined with celestial jewels, he held court over the Olympian assembly. Beneath its vaulted canopy, gods feasted, debated, and shaped the fates of mortals. From this height, Zeus loosed his thunderbolts and proclaimed his judgments, his voice rolling across the heavens and into the hearts of men.

These sacred structures were more than dwellings—they were living expressions of heavenly beings. In their perfect design, they mirrored the gods themselves: eternal, radiant, and indivisible from the forces they commanded. To walk among them was to step into a realm where form and power were one, and every pillar, gate, and stone hummed with the song of creation.

Symbol of Divine Authority

Mount Olympus stood as the supreme emblem of sacred authority—a summit whose unchanging presence mirrored the gods' eternal dominion and separation from the mortal realm. To the ancient Greeks, its towering form evoked the ever-watchful presence of the Olympians, whose will stirred both the fall of rain and the rise of empires. From the heights of Olympus, the gods governed the cosmos, shaping the currents of fate with hands unseen yet ever felt.

The mountain was not merely a dwelling, but the throne of celestial rule. Within its radiant courts, the gods gathered to render judgment, forge decrees, and maintain the sacred balance of order. These god-forged councils thundered with consequence, as immortals debated justice, destiny, and the mortal lives entangled in their designs. Olympus became the crucible of divine intent, where harmony was pursued even as immortal tempers flared.

Its symbolic might resounded in myths such as that of the Trojan War, born from a fateful contest between Hera, Athena, and Aphrodite. Though the judgment of Paris occurred upon Mount Ida, its ripples reached Olympus, where the gods chose sides and shaped the war's tide. Here, the mountain's authority was revealed not in isolation, but in influence—its mythic summit echoing across battlefields and into the hearts of heroes.

Olympus's image was carved into the rituals of Greek life, its name invoked in prayer, oath, and sacrifice. To entreat the gods of Olympus was to bow before the highest power, to seek favor from the eternal watchers above. Through sacred festivals and solemn rites, mortals renewed their bond with the divine, ever mindful of the mountain's gaze.

In poetry and art, Olympus rose in radiant splendor—depicted by Homer, Hesiod, and countless others as a realm of brilliance and perfect order. It offered a vision beyond suffering, a celestial ideal untouched by the turmoil of the human world. Its constancy became a metaphor for sacred truth, a still point in the turning world.

With its shining gates, immortal palaces, and seat among the stars, Mount Olympus was not simply the backdrop of myth—it was the embodiment of god-forged supremacy. In its enduring grandeur, the Greeks found more than myth; they found meaning. Olympus was the heart of the heavens, the nexus where god and mortal fate intertwined, and the eternal testament to the power that shaped the cosmos.

MOUNTAIN SHAPES A CIVILIZATION

The majesty of Mount Olympus transcended myth, embedding itself in the very soul of Greek culture. It stood not only as the dwelling of gods but as a sacred pillar of religious devotion, artistic creation, and collective identity. From towering temples raised in its honor to solemn rituals invoking its divine inhabitants, Olympus became the spiritual heart of a civilization seeking harmony with the heavens. Artists and poets gave it form and voice, rendering its splendor in stone and verse. Across generations, its legacy endured—as a symbol of transcendence, a muse for the imagination, and an eternal bridge between mortal longing and sacred truth.

*"And the gods sat upon the golden floor
of Olympus, where they feasted,
and all their halls were filled
with light and laughter."*
— Homer, The Iliad

Worship in the Shadow of Olympus

The towering majesty of Mount Olympus stirred devotion across the Greek world, inspiring the rise of monumental temples and sacred rites that echoed its celestial presence. Though its peak was deemed unreachable—a realm reserved for the immortals—its heavenly influence descended into valleys and cities, shaping the spiritual rhythm of ancient life.

Foremost among these sanctuaries stood the Temple of Zeus at Olympia, a marvel hewn in stone to honor the king of the gods. Within its hallowed walls, the god's likeness towered—an ivory and gold colossus wrought by the hand of Phidias. Seated in royal splendor, scepter in hand, crowned by the eagle of heaven, Zeus radiated majesty. Pilgrims traveled from every corner of Greece to stand in reverent awe, drawn to the earthly echo of Olympus's might.

The rituals held in his honor were no less grand. Sacrifices, processions, and solemn rites served as bridges between mortal devotion and immortal favor. The Olympic Games, born at his altar, were as sacred as they were glorious—beginning with offerings and oaths sworn before the flame of Olympus. Through these ceremonies, the athletes did not merely compete; they communed with the gods, their struggle an act of homage.

Beyond Zeus, the other Olympians received their due—Hera's grace, Athena's wisdom, Poseidon's command—all celebrated in festivals adorned with chants, dances, and prayer. These rites affirmed the gods' dominion over war and harvest, sky and sea, and bound the people in shared reverence beneath their gaze.

Even the voice of prophecy was linked to Olympus's sacred weight. At Dodona, the oldest oracle of Zeus, priests listened to the whispering oaks, interpreting their rustling leaves as the breath of the god. Pilgrims sought truths from the ethereal summit, believing Olympus was not distant, but near—present in wind and word.

Through temple, ritual, and sacred vow, Mount Olympus reigned not only in myth but in the hearts of its people—a beacon of divine presence, where the eternal met the earthly in flame, stone, and sacred song.

Echoes of Olympus in Art and Verse

The grandeur of Mount Olympus found eternal life in Greek art and literature, where it rose not only as the dwelling of the gods but as a symbol of the immortal itself. Its image, both radiant and remote, became a vessel through which artists and poets revealed the majesty, power, and mystery of the immortals who ruled from its heights.

In sculpture and painting, Olympus was envisioned as a realm of light and perfection, where the gods dwelled in eternal harmony. The Olympians appeared in forms of idealized beauty, their features chiseled with divine grace, their bodies bearing the elegance of immortality. They were shown amidst clouds or within gilded halls, their surroundings imbued with splendor befitting the mountain's sacred renown. These images inspired awe and reverence, portraying the gods as beings beyond reach, yet ever present in vision and spirit.

In the epics of Homer, Olympus loomed large. The *Iliad* and the *Odyssey* portrayed it as the seat of celestial will, where gods convened to steer the course of mortal destiny. From its shining heights, Zeus and his kin passed judgment, their decrees shaping the rise and fall of heroes and cities. Olympus was not a silent backdrop—it was a force within the tale, its influence stretching from heavenly halls to blood-stained battlefields.

In *Theogony*, Hesiod gave the mountain its mythic crown. His verses traced the gods' emergence and their enthronement upon Olympus, where chaos yielded to divine order. In his telling, the mountain stood as the axis of the cosmos, a bastion where law, harmony, and sovereignty were forged. Olympus, thus, became the eternal symbol of structure and balance in a universe once wild and formless.

Yet Olympus was more than myth—it was metaphor. Poets and philosophers alike saw in its soaring peak a mirror of human longing. As the gods reigned from on high, so too did mortals seek to rise—to transcend weakness, to strive for excellence, to approach the gods through wisdom, valor, or art. Olympus became a symbol not only of the gods' perfection, but of humanity's quest to touch the sacred.

Through brushstroke, verse, and thought, Olympus endured— as image, as ideal, and as inspiration. In every expression, it reflected the highest aspirations of a people who saw in the heavens not only their gods, but their own path toward greatness.

Olympus Reborn in Modern Myth

The legacy of Mount Olympus has echoed far beyond the marble temples and oral traditions of ancient Greece, ascending into the heart of modern storytelling. Its myths and symbols—timeless and transcendent—continue to breathe life into literature, film, and philosophy, captivating the imagination across cultures and eras. Olympus endures as a beacon of the heavens and the extraordinary, its silhouette etched into the collective consciousness.

In today's literature, Olympus often emerges as a threshold between worlds—a gateway into the fantastical. Writers of fantasy and science fiction draw upon its ancient grandeur to craft realms where mortals walk among gods and fate bends to Olympian will. Rick Riordan's *Percy Jackson* series reimagines Olympus as a skyborne palace above New York City, blending myth with modernity and introducing a new generation to the immortal tales of the Olympians. Through such retellings, the old gods speak anew, their relevance rekindled for a changing world.

Film and television, too, have embraced Olympus's eternal pull. Epic sagas like *Clash of the Titans* and *Hercules* summon its radiant halls and tempestuous deities to the screen, casting Olympus as both wonder and battleground. These portrayals explore the tension between immortal decree and human defiance, mirroring the ancient question: how does one navigate a world shaped by powers beyond comprehension?

Yet Olympus's influence is not confined to fiction. In philosophy and psychology, the mountain rises as a symbol of aspiration—of the climb toward greatness, truth, and inner order. It becomes a metaphor for the soul's ascent, for the human pursuit of purpose and transcendence. To dream of Olympus is to dream of reaching the summit of one's potential.

The myths rooted in its heights continue to probe the nature of power, justice, and flawed divinity. The Olympian gods—with all their triumphs and tempests—reflect the complexity of the human condition. Their stories challenge us to question, to reflect, and to strive. In this way, Mount Olympus remains more than myth—it is a mirror, a mountaintop of meaning, and an eternal bridge between the mortal and the divine.

AT THE HEART OF MYTH

Mount Olympus is far more than a soaring summit of stone— it is the throne of the gods, the sacred heart of Greek mythology, and a timeless symbol of ethereal majesty. From its cloud-crowned heights, the Olympians gazed down upon the mortal world, weaving the fates of gods and men with unseen threads of power and will.

In this journey, we have ascended its mythic slopes—beholding the splendor of its golden palaces, the rituals that bound mortals to immortals, and the enduring presence it held in the hearts of the ancient Greeks. Olympus was not merely a realm of residence, but a mirror of divine order, where harmony and rivalry coexisted in eternal tension.

At the center of this radiant domain stood Zeus—the thunder-wielding sovereign whose rule shaped the balance of heaven and earth. As king of the gods, his authority defined Olympus, and his voice echoed across both celestial and mortal realms. In the chapter that follows, we turn our gaze to Zeus himself: his rise from rebellion to reign, the power he wielded, and the legends that forged his legacy as the unchallenged ruler of Olympus.

CHAPTER 2

ZEUS

King of the Gods

The myth of Zeus weaves a timeless tapestry of rebellion, triumph, and god-forged rule—charting his rise from a hidden child to the undisputed sovereign of the gods. Rescued from the fate that claimed his siblings, Zeus grew in secret, destined to challenge Cronus and the tyranny of the old order. Through the storm and fire of the Titanomachy, he emerged as a force of cosmic renewal, wielding thunder to break the chains of the past. As king of Olympus, Zeus became the guardian of law and balance, his rule anchoring both mortal fate and immortal order. His legacy forged the foundation upon which all Olympian power stands.

"Zeus, the father of gods and men,
whose thunder shakes the heavens,
and whose will guides the fates of all."
— Homer, The Iliad

Ascent of Zeus

Long before Zeus hurled bolt of lightning or ruled from his golden throne atop Olympus, the cosmos lay under a shadow of tyranny. Cronus, king of the Titans, reigned through fear—his power born in betrayal. At Gaia's urging, he had overthrown Uranus, his own father. But with his fall, Uranus cast a chilling prophecy: one day, a child of Cronus would rise against him, just as he had risen against his own sire.

This curse festered in Cronus's mind, twisting love into dread. When Rhea, his sister and queen, bore him children—Hestia,

Demeter, Hera, Hades, and Poseidon—Cronus swallowed them at birth, imprisoning their sacred essence within himself. Grief-stricken and unwilling to surrender another child, Rhea hatched a bold deception.

When Zeus was born, she spirited him away to a hidden cave on Crete and wrapped a stone in cloth. Cronus, blinded by terror, devoured the decoy without pause. In secret, the infant god was nurtured by nymphs and suckled by Amalthea, the divine goat whose milk infused him with celestial strength. To conceal his cries, the Curetes—bronze-clad guardians—clashed their swords in rhythmic war-dance, echoing through the cavern like a shield against fate.

Zeus grew swiftly in power and purpose. Upon reaching manhood, he turned to Metis, the goddess of wisdom, who guided him in crafting a plan to overthrow the tyrant. Disguised, Zeus approached Cronus and offered a potion brewed by Metis's cunning hand. The drink was laced with primordial force. Upon tasting it, Cronus convulsed and vomited forth the gods he had once consumed.

Freed at last, Zeus's siblings rose beside him—not as scattered heirs, but as an Olympian legion. Their fury ignited the heavens, and together they launched a rebellion that would fracture the old world and give birth to a new divine order.

War of the Titans

What followed was the Titanomachy—a war of cosmic fury and mythic reckoning. Zeus and his liberated siblings, now called the Olympians, rose against Cronus and the ancient Titans in a ten-year siege for dominion over the cosmos. The sky thundered, the earth split, and the seas raged as immortal forces collided in a struggle that shook creation to its roots.

At first, the Titans stood unyielding, their colossal strength and ancient might matching the young gods blow for blow. Yet Zeus, both shrewd and bold, sought power hidden beyond the battlefield. He descended into Tartarus, the abyss where Cronus had imprisoned the Hecatoncheires and the Cyclopes. The Hecatoncheires, giants of terrifying form, bore a hundred arms and fifty heads. The Cyclopes, one-eyed and eternal, were master smiths of celestial weaponry. Zeus broke their chains—and in doing so, turned the tide of fate.

Grateful for their freedom, the Cyclopes forged weapons of unimaginable power. To Zeus, they gave the thunderbolt, a weapon of sky-born wrath. To Poseidon, the trident, capable of stirring oceans and cracking the earth. To Hades, the helm of darkness, which cloaked him in shadow and silence. Armed with these sacred gifts, the Olympians surged with newfound strength.

Zeus released lightning that split the heavens, igniting the firmament in blinding fire. Poseidon summoned tsunamis and quakes to rend the Titans' ranks. Hades, veiled in invisibility, sowed terror in the enemy's heart. The Hecatoncheires hurled boulders like falling stars, their relentless assault shaking the very bones of the world.

In the war's final clash, Cronus was cast down, and the Titans defeated. Bound in unbreakable chains, they were hurled into Tartarus, now guarded by the very beings they once imprisoned. Victory belonged to the Olympians.

To consecrate their triumph, the gods claimed Mount Olympus as their celestial seat. Upon its radiant peak, they built their golden halls and established a new god-forged order. Zeus, crowned by thunder and glory, ascended the throne as king of gods and guardian of balance—his reign marking the dawn of a new era.

Lord of Justice and Oath

As king of the gods, Zeus bore the sacred mantle of arbiter of justice, a divine overseer entrusted with preserving balance in a world forever leaning toward chaos. From his golden throne atop Olympus, he cast his gaze across heaven and earth, weighing the deeds of mortals and immortals alike. His decrees shaped the fate of the cosmos, and his will was the axis upon which order turned.

Zeus's justice inspired awe and dread. He was guardian of oaths, protector of the sacred law, and avenger of broken truths. To the ancient Greeks, he embodied dike—the principle of rightful order. His bolts were not mere weapons of wrath but emblems of celestial retribution, falling like heavenly verdicts upon those who defied the harmony of the gods.

Among the most enduring tales of Zeus's judgment is that of Prometheus, the fire-bringer. In compassion for humanity, Prometheus stole flame from Olympus and delivered it to mortals—a gift of light and defiance. Enraged by this rebellion, Zeus chained the Titan to a desolate cliff, condemning him to endless torment beneath the wings of an eagle that devoured his liver by day, only for it to regenerate by night. This sentence was not cruelty, but a lesson carved in agony: the will of Zeus must not be defied.

Yet divine justice was not without compassion. Zeus watched over the righteous and the humble. In the tale of Baucis and Philemon, he walked the earth disguised as a traveler and found kindness in a poor couple's modest home. In reward for their hospitality, he transformed their cottage into a temple and granted them the grace to live—and die—as one. Through such mercy, Zeus revealed the dual nature of justice: stern in judgment, generous in grace.

Even among gods, Zeus held the scales. He mediated their quarrels and curbed their rivalries, ensuring that Olympian discord did not fracture the fabric of existence. During the Trojan War, his decisions wove through the ambitions of Hera, Athena, and Aphrodite, balancing immortal desires with mortal fate. His hand guided the storm, but also the stillness after.

In the arc of his life—from hidden child to ruler of Olympus— Zeus became more than a conqueror; he became a keeper of cosmic order. His story is the mythic reflection of justice itself— both thunder and shelter, wrath and reward—an eternal testament to the power that binds gods and mortals to the same sacred thread.

MIGHT OF THE IMMORTAL KING

The powers of Zeus embody the vastness of his dominion, revealing a god whose authority spans sky and storm, law and fate, wrath and grace. As master of thunder and lightning, he wielded the heavens as both shield and spear—his celestial fire igniting the sky as emblems of divine will. Yet his strength reached far beyond the tempest. Zeus was the enforcer of cosmic justice, the guardian of order in a universe ever on the edge of chaos. He moved through the world with transformative force, taking many forms— beast, flame, and mist—to guide, test, or seduce. Each expression of his power struck a balance between might and mercy, creation and judgment. Through these sacred forces, Zeus reigned not only as king of Olympus but as the eternal heart of myth itself, his presence echoing across the ages.

> *"Zeus, who marshals the thunderheads,*
> *lord of lightning,*
> *master of the raging storm."*
> — Homer, The Iliad

Thunder That Crowned the Sky

The boundless sky was Zeus's dominion, and through thunder, lightning, and storm, he revealed the majesty of his mythic power. From his throne atop Olympus, he ruled the heavens with awe-inspiring command, wielding the elements not as forces of nature, but as extensions of his will. A thunderstorm under Zeus's gaze became a sacred proclamation—his fury splitting the sky, his mercy descending as rain upon a thirsty earth.

The thunderbolt, his signature weapon, was no mere flame hurled from the clouds. Forged by the Cyclopes in gratitude for their liberation from Tartarus, it bore the primal energy of the cosmos itself. With a single motion, Zeus could summon fire from the firmament, shattering peaks, igniting forests, and silencing defiance in gods and mortals alike. It was not just a weapon—it was judgment made visible.

Yet the power of Zeus was not bound to ruin. He commanded the rain that nourished the soil, sustained the harvest, and preserved the lives of those who honored him. Farmers lifted prayers skyward, seeking the favor of the storm-bringer whose waters meant survival. His storms bore the dual promise of destruction and renewal, revealing him as both harbinger of wrath and giver of life—a god of thunder, but also of fertility.

Myths abound that echo his elemental dominion. Among them is the tale of Salmoneus, a mortal king whose arrogance led him to mimic the lord of lightning. With chariots and fire, he dared to feign the thunder of Zeus. In swift response, the god cast a true bolt from the heavens, obliterating the imposter and proving that the sky bowed to no mortal will.

For the Greeks, the sky was more than air and cloud—it was a celestial canvas where Zeus wrote his will in storm and silence. A crack of thunder could stir armies or still hearts. The heavens, ever shifting and vast, mirrored the god who ruled them: powerful, unpredictable, and eternal.

Keeper of Balance and Order

Zeus's dominion reached far beyond storm and sky—it extended into the invisible threads that bound the universe. As enforcer of god-forged law and guardian of moral order, he upheld the harmony between gods and mortals, ensuring that chaos never overtook creation. His power was not brute force alone, but a sacred duty to maintain the balance that sustained the cosmos.

Among the immortals, Zeus reigned with unquestioned authority. Though his fellow Olympians wielded vast powers, it was he who preserved unity on Mount Olympus. Seated upon his high throne, he presided over divine councils, settling disputes and tempering ambition with wisdom. Myths speak of his might when Hera, Athena, and Poseidon conspired against him—how he quelled their rebellion and reasserted the sacred order, a reminder that Olympus stood firm only beneath his rule.

Among mortals, Zeus was the sanctifier of oaths and the avenger of broken vows. To swear by Zeus was to invoke the highest sacred bond; to break that vow was to summon his wrath. The Furies, relentless agents of vengeance, moved at his behest, tracking those who defied the moral fabric he upheld. Justice, in Zeus's realm, was not suggestion—it was law, woven into the stars.

The myth of Sisyphus echoes Zeus's unforgiving judgment. The cunning king who mocked death and defied the gods was sentenced to an eternal labor—forever pushing a stone uphill, only to watch it fall again. His punishment was not mere cruelty, but an eternal reminder that no mortal could outwit the will of Olympus.

Yet Zeus's justice was not blind to virtue. He protected the weak, rewarded the faithful, and punished betrayal where it struck deepest. When Ixion violated the sacred laws of hospitality—xenia—Zeus bound him to a wheel of fire, turning endlessly in the heavens. But in the tale of Deucalion and Pyrrha, Zeus saw righteousness and spared them from the flood, allowing them to rebuild humanity in the light of renewal.

Zeus's hand did not weigh with tyranny, but with balance. His power was the fulcrum between chaos and order, and his rule preserved the harmony of both immortal and mortal worlds. Through punishment and mercy alike, he remained the eternal judge—stern, watchful, and just.

Forms of the Unseen God

Among the many powers that set Zeus apart was his gift of transformation—the ability to take on any form he desired. Through shapeshifting, he moved between realms seen and unseen, cloaked in cloud or creature, veiled in beauty or humility. This divine mutability granted him access to mortal lives and immortal affairs alike, allowing him to influence destiny with cunning, subtlety, and power.

The myths of his transformations are among the most storied in all of Greek lore. To woo Leda, he became a radiant swan, gliding across still waters with an otherworldly grace. For Europa, he took the form of a gentle white bull, so serene and noble that she climbed upon his back—only to be borne across the sea into legend. These were not tricks of the flesh, but acts of ethereal artistry—each form chosen to bypass resistance and fulfill intent.

Yet shapeshifting was not reserved for seduction alone. Zeus often walked the earth in humble guise, cloaked as a beggar, wanderer, or stranger. In these forms, he tested the hearts of mortals—offering kindness and judgment in equal measure. Those who welcomed the unknown were rewarded; those who scorned the sacred guest brought ruin upon themselves. His transformations bridged the gap between heaven and earth, allowing him to walk among his creations without the burden of revelation.

His interventions, though often veiled in personal desire, shaped the fates of many. In the tale of Io, he transformed her into a heifer to shield her from Hera's wrath, an act of protection that spiraled into sorrow and exile. Such stories reveal the layered nature of Zeus's will—at once protective and possessive, divine and fallible.

In his shifting form, Zeus mirrored the cosmos itself—ever-changing, vast, and unpredictable. Just as storms roll from clear skies, so too could the king of the gods emerge in any shape, his presence felt in wind and feather, flame and stranger's voice. His power to transform was not merely a tool, but a reflection of the paradox at the heart of divinity: omnipotent yet intimate, distant yet always near.

Through thunder and storm, judgment and disguise, Zeus's powers did more than command—they shaped the myths, the world, and the eternal dance between the mortal and immortal.

MARBLE AND MYTH

Zeus's profound influence on Greek culture echoed through the grand temples built in his honor, the sacred festivals that bound cities in shared devotion, and the ideals of kingship and justice he came to embody. His presence was felt in the towering sanctuary at Olympia and the whispering oaks of Dodona, where gods and mortals met in prayer and prophecy. More than a sky god, Zeus stood as the divine symbol of order, wisdom, and rightful rule. Through worship, myth, and law, he shaped the spiritual, social, and political fabric of ancient Greece, becoming a timeless figure of reverence and authority.

> *"Zeus, who thunders on high, the king of gods and men, whose decrees are eternal, and whose will none may defy."*
> — *Hesiod, Theogony*

Halls of Storm and Whisper

The earthly presence of Zeus's majesty was etched into the sacred architecture of ancient Greece, rising in stone and spirit through temples built to honor his celestial power. These sanctuaries were far more than places of ritual—they were testaments to Zeus's supreme stature among the gods and to the reverence of those who sought his favor. Among the most renowned were Olympia and Dodona, each reflecting a different aspect of his rule: one in grandeur and strength, the other in mystery and counsel.

At Olympia, the Temple of Zeus stood as a triumph of ancient craftsmanship and devotion. Within its towering columns rested one of the Seven Wonders of the Ancient World—a statue of Zeus so immense and radiant that to gaze upon it was to feel the presence of the divine. Seated upon a majestic throne, Zeus held the figure of Nike, goddess of victory, in one hand and a scepter crowned with an eagle—the symbol of his dominion—in the other. Fashioned from ivory and gold, the statue shimmered with an ethereal brilliance, embodying Zeus not merely as a deity, but as the supreme arbiter of gods and men.

Dodona, by contrast, was a place of quiet awe, nestled in a grove of sacred oaks where Zeus spoke not through stone, but through the wind. Here, he was worshipped as Zeus Naios, lord of the tree, and Zeus Bouleus, giver of counsel. Pilgrims journeyed to this ancient oracle to seek answers whispered through the rustling leaves. Priestesses and priests listened closely, interpreting the murmurs of nature as the voice of the god himself. In this sacred grove, Zeus's wisdom flowed not in thunder but in breath and breeze.

Together, Olympia and Dodona stood as pillars of faith and identity for the Greek world. One proclaimed Zeus's might in marble and gold; the other his presence in rustling leaves and sacred speech. Each offered a gateway between mortal and immortal, reinforcing the god's enduring role as both ruler and guide in the hearts of the people.

Sacred Games and Devotion

Zeus's worship was deeply woven into the spiritual and cultural rhythms of ancient Greek life, from solemn rites of sacrifice to grand festivals that celebrated his dominion over gods and men. These acts of devotion reflected not only reverence, but a sacred bond between mortals and the divine. Among the most revered of these celebrations were the Olympic Games, held in the god's honor at Olympia—a fusion of athletic glory and religious piety that captured the heart of the Hellenic world.

Every four years, the Olympic Games summoned athletes from across the Greek city-states, each bearing the hope of victory beneath the gaze of Zeus. Before the contests began, a sacred truce—ekecheiria—was declared, halting all wars and honoring Zeus as the bringer of peace and order. The competitions, from foot races to chariot battles, were not mere sport—they were living offerings, demonstrations of strength and excellence made to please the god. Sacrifices at the Altar of Zeus, built from centuries of ash and bone, marked the start of the games. Victors were crowned with olive wreaths, a symbol of heavenly favor, their triumphs seen as signs of Zeus's blessing and judgment.

Beyond Olympia, Zeus was honored in festivals across the land. In Athens, the Diasia celebrated Zeus Meilichios, the merciful aspect of the god. Offerings of animal-shaped cakes were made to seek forgiveness and invoke his gentle protection. In rural regions, he was venerated as the guardian of fields and flocks, with prayers rising to the heavens for rain, harvest, and fertility. Whether as ruler, peacemaker, or nurturer, Zeus was ever present in the cycles of life.

These festivals and rituals did more than pay tribute—they united communities under a shared devotion and affirmed the sacred order Zeus upheld. In sacrifice and celebration, in prayer and performance, the Greeks gave voice to their reverence, binding themselves to the god who reigned from sky and summit alike.

Throne of Power

As king of the gods, Zeus stood as the divine archetype of leadership, a model that ancient Greek rulers sought to emulate in strength, justice, and the preservation of order. His myths served not only as sacred tales but as a blueprint for governance, offering a vision of power tempered by wisdom and guided by law.

Zeus's rule was marked by might, yet anchored in balance. Though unrivaled in strength, he governed with discernment, often choosing mediation over force. His ability to resolve immortal disputes—sometimes with thunder, sometimes with wisdom—reflected an ideal that mortal kings aspired to: firm but fair, commanding yet just. In Greek society, this became the gold standard of rulership—power wielded not for dominion alone, but for the welfare of the realm.

Central to Zeus's influence was his role as the protector of oaths and enforcer of sacred law. To break one's word was to offend the gods, and especially Zeus, whose authority upheld the moral contract between rulers and the ruled. A leader's vow, sworn in his name, was no mere promise—it was a bond bound to divine justice. Integrity, under Zeus's watch, was not optional but essential.

The thunderbolt, Zeus's emblem of sovereignty, symbolized not only destructive wrath but the weight of command. To invoke it was to claim both reverence and responsibility. Leaders who aligned themselves with this imagery understood that power, if misused, could bring ruin as swiftly as it could secure peace.

Even in democratic Athens, where rule was shared among citizens, Zeus's influence endured. The city's legal and ethical foundations were shaped by the principles he embodied—dike, justice; eunomia, good order. These values ensured that leadership was shaped not by personal ambition, but by a higher standard rooted in fairness and divine order.

Through his myths and worship, Zeus offered more than celestial rulership—he offered a living ideal. To the Greeks, he was both sovereign of the heavens and a mirror of what mortal leadership could be: just, wise, and resolute. In Zeus, power found its conscience, and kings found their guide.

ETERNAL REIGN OF ZEUS

Zeus, the thunder-wielding sovereign of Mount Olympus, remains one of the most commanding and enigmatic figures in all of Greek mythology. His tale—marked by mythic triumphs, cosmic judgment, and mortal entanglements—reveals a god of vast contradictions: wise yet fallible, just yet unforgiving, supreme yet bound by the threads of fate. In Zeus, the Greeks envisioned not perfection, but the full spectrum of celestial authority.

We have traced his ascent from a hidden cave in Crete to the golden throne of Olympus, where his victory over the Titans crowned him ruler of gods and men. His command of thunder and sky affirmed his celestial dominion, while his role as the enforcer of sacred justice upheld the balance between chaos and order. Through shapeshifting and intervention, he moved among mortals unseen, guiding destinies and shaping legend with every step.

Yet Zeus's reign was far from serene. His passions, rivalries, and unyielding will often sparked the very myths that shaped Greek belief, revealing a god revered not for flawless virtue, but for immense power and the burden it carried. Even amid discord, Zeus maintained the divine order, his rule binding the Olympians under law and decree.

As our gaze shifts from Zeus, king of the gods, we turn now to Hera, his queen and equal in majesty. Far more than a consort, Hera emerges as a force of will and purpose, a guardian of sacred vows and protector of family and legacy. In the chapter ahead, we will step into her world—one of dignity, defiance, and numinous sovereignty—and discover the strength of the goddess who reigned beside the storm.

CHAPTER 3

HERA

Queen of the Gods

Hera's myth reveals a goddess of sovereign grace and unyielding resolve. Born of Cronus and Rhea, she rose to Olympus as the guardian of marriage, honor, and sanctified order. Her union with Zeus, marked by betrayal, ignited a righteous fury that defended what was holy. Jealous yet just, proud yet protective, Hera embodied the trials of ethereal love and the dignity of immortal rule. Through storm and silence, she stood unwavering— a symbol of sacred vows, fierce loyalty, and the enduring strength of a queen crowned by both wrath and devotion.

> *"Hera, golden-throned, immortal queen,*
> *bride of great Zeus,*
> *you whose province is the wide heaven,*
> *and whose realm is the earth and the sea."*
> — *Homeric Hymn to Hera*

Making of a Queen

Hera's origins were as noble and ancient as the heavens she would one day rule. Born to Cronus and Rhea, she entered a world steeped in prophecy and unrest. Like her Olympian siblings— Hestia, Demeter, Hades, and Poseidon—Hera was swallowed at birth by her father, who, fearing his downfall, sought to imprison fate itself within his body. Yet destiny stirred. When Zeus rose in defiance of Cronus, he freed his engulfed kin, and Hera emerged not as a child, but as a radiant goddess, her spirit forged in silence and strength.

In the dawn of the Olympian reign, Hera's presence brought order and majesty. Zeus, struck by her beauty and regality, pursued her not with thunder, but with cunning. In one tale, he became a trembling cuckoo bird, caught in storm and sorrow. Hera, moved by compassion, took the creature to her breast—only for Zeus to reveal his true form. Bound by fate and softened by persistence, she consented, and their union was sealed in a divine wedding celebrated by all the gods.

Yet their marriage was no fairy tale. Crowned as queen of Olympus, Hera ruled beside Zeus with pride and purpose, but his betrayals pierced the sanctity of their bond. Her jealousy, fierce and legendary, was not born of vanity, but of wounded honor. Through their turbulent union, Hera's myth deepened—not merely as wife or consort, but as a sovereign force who upheld the pure, bore the weight of betrayal, and reigned with unshaken dignity.

Jealousy and Wrath

Though often cast in a harsh light, Hera's jealousy was born not of vanity, but of wounded pride and spiritual purpose. As the guardian of marriage, her fury rose not merely from betrayal, but from Zeus's countless affairs—with goddesses, nymphs, and mortal women alike—that mocked the vows she upheld. Her wrath, though fearsome, was the fire of a queen unwilling to be diminished, and through it came some of the most enduring tales in Greek myth.

Among these is the tale of Io, a mortal maiden who drew Zeus's gaze. To conceal his desire, Zeus veiled her in the form of a white heifer. Yet Hera, ever watchful, saw through the ruse and demanded the creature as a gift. Bound by suspicion and unable to refuse, Zeus complied. Hera entrusted Io to Argus Panoptes, the hundred-eyed sentinel who never fully slept. When Hermes, at Zeus's behest, slew Argus, Hera mourned her loyal servant by setting his eyes in the tail of the peacock—her sacred bird, forever bearing the memory of vigilance. But her vengeance did not rest. She unleashed a gadfly to torment Io, driving her across distant lands in agony, until at last, Zeus restored her form and freedom.

No myth more deeply reflects Hera's unyielding rage than the life of Heracles, the mighty son of Zeus and the mortal Alcmene. From his birth, Hera's anger pursued him. She sent serpents to his cradle, yet even as an infant, Heracles crushed them with immortal strength. Throughout his life, she wove trials and torments into his path, none greater than the madness she summoned, which drove him to a tragic crime—slaying his own wife and children. From this sorrow rose his redemption: the Twelve Labors, feats so harrowing they forged his legend in fire and endurance. In her opposition, Hera shaped the very trials that proved his greatness.

Beneath the surface of these myths lies a portrait of Hera not as cruel, but as complex—a goddess whose anger echoed with dignity and defiance. She fought not for dominance, but for respect. Her vengeance was the voice of a queen who would not be cast aside, a heaven-wrought power unwilling to be silenced, and through that fire, her legend burned ever brighter.

Guardian of Oaths Unbroken

Though her fury could shake the heavens, Hera was equally revered as the spiritual guardian of marriage and the hallowed architect of the household. To the ancient Greeks, she embodied fidelity, endurance, and the sanctity of the marital bond. Her presence was invoked at wedding ceremonies through solemn prayers and sacred rites, her blessing believed to bring harmony, prosperity, and divine protection to those who honored her laws.

This reverence found vivid expression in the Heraia Festival, celebrated in her name at Olympia. Women competed in athletic games, running not for conquest, but for grace, strength, and the favor of their goddess. These contests honored Hera's own sacred vigor and symbolized her connection to women's dignity, virtue, and endurance. Rituals and offerings marked the day, reaffirming her place as patroness of domestic life and the guiding voice within the home.

In myth, Hera's devotion to marriage stood in stark contrast to Zeus's betrayals, casting her not as submissive consort, but as a figure of unwavering commitment. Though her own marriage bore the scars of sorrow, she remained steadfast in her duty—upholding union where others might abandon it. Hera endured, not out of weakness, but out of reverence for the vows she protected, becoming a mirror of mortal resilience.

Her influence reached beyond Olympus into the mortal realm. In the tale of Jason and Medea, it was Hera who favored Jason's quest for the Golden Fleece and subtly guided the union. Though that story ended in tragedy, her early support revealed her desire to see love sanctified under her watchful gaze. Hera did not shape every outcome, but she stood as witness and protector to those who honored her privileged trust.

Beyond the wedding altar, Hera's mantle extended to women in all stages of life. As a goddess of motherhood, she was called upon in childbirth, her temples housing spaces where women prayed for safe deliveries and the strength to raise their families. Though her emotions burned with intensity, they reflected a deep kinship with mortal experience—love, pain, pride, and perseverance.

In Hera, the Greeks saw not only a queen, but a goddess who bore the weight of devotion and the trials of love. Through flame and fidelity, vengeance and virtue, she reigned as a symbol of the enduring strength that binds families, sanctifies vows, and gives divine voice to the complexities of the human heart.

SACRED AUTHORITY

Hera's powers flowed from her blessed dominion over marriage, family, and the cycles of womanhood. As the divine matron of vows and births, she bestowed harmony upon households and watched over the rites of union and childbirth with solemn grace. Yet beneath her nurturing mantle stirred a fierce, unrelenting will— one that punished betrayal and guarded oaths with thunderous conviction. Her ire was not chaos, but justice; her blessings, not indulgent, but earned. In this spiritual balance of compassion and retribution, Hera reigned as a goddess of towering presence and sacred authority—unchallenged in pride, enduring in power.

> *"Hera, whose eye sees all,*
> *and whose wrath none may escape,*
> *guards the sanctity of marriage and*
> *the bonds of the family."*
> *— Homeric Hymn to Hera*

Empress of Hearthbound Ties

In the spiritual weave of Greek mythology, Hera reigned as the divine heart of marriage and the guardian of family. As queen of Olympus, her very name was synonymous with matrimony, and her presence sanctified the vows exchanged between mortal souls.

More than a figure of fidelity, Hera was a celestial guide—bestowing grace, endurance, and solemn blessing upon unions forged in love and duty. Her favor was sought not through grand gestures, but through intimate rites—prayers whispered at altars, garlands laid before her image, and bridal hair offered in pure devotion.

To the ancient Greeks, marriage was the pillar of civilization, and through Hera, this union became sacred. Though her own marriage to Zeus was marked by storm, it stood as a celestial archetype—a testament to resilience amid conflict. Brides invoked her name for strength; households honored her for peace. In festivals held in her honor, mortals gathered not only to celebrate but to connect with a goddess who did not dwell above their struggles, but walked beside them as a patron of life's most personal covenants.

Hera's influence flowed beyond the bridal chamber into the hearth. As divine mother of the Olympians, she understood the trials of family and the burdens of love. She mediated quarrels among gods, just as mortal women looked to her for wisdom in raising children and maintaining harmony within their homes. Through her steadfast patronage, Hera embodied the sanctity of loyalty, the strength of tradition, and the enduring power of love woven into the fabric of family.

Womanhood and Birth

Hera's dominion reached deep into the heart of womanhood, governing the hallowed transitions from maiden to bride, and from mother to matron. As queen of Olympus and sovereign of the household, her influence touched every pivotal moment in a woman's life—marriage, conception, and the perilous threshold of birth. Though Artemis was more closely tied to the act of delivery, Hera's power over childbirth ran through the fabric of family itself, woven into the preservation of lineage, legacy, and maternal strength.

Her role in childbirth was often veiled in symbolism and expressed through both protection and trial. As mother to Ares, Hebe, Hephaestus, and Eileithyia—the goddess of childbirth—Hera knew well the labor of motherhood and the fierce devotion it demanded. Women invoked her blessing for fertility, safe passage through labor, and strength in raising the next generation. Her sanctuaries, adorned with votive offerings and whispered prayers, stood as havens for those seeking heavenly favor in their most vulnerable hours.

Yet Hera's power over birth could just as swiftly shift from blessing to burden. When scorned, she wielded her influence as a weapon, as in the tale of Leto—beloved of Zeus and bearer of Apollo and Artemis. Enraged by the affair, Hera forbade any land beneath the sun to shelter the laboring goddess. Only the drifting island of Delos, unmoored and unclaimed, offered refuge. Even then, Hera stalled the birth by withholding Eileithyia's aid, commanding delay through celestial will. Only through the intervention of the gods did Leto give birth, her suffering sanctified by the greatness of the children she bore.

In such stories, Hera emerges not merely as a goddess of nurture, but as the force behind life's greatest threshold. She could open the gates of fertility or seal them in silence. Her presence in childbirth mirrored the nature of birth itself—blessed, mysterious, and fraught with risk. To Greek women, Hera was not a distant mythic ideal, but a powerful presence—capable of compassion or challenge—whose blessing was sought and whose wrath was feared at the turning points of life.

Fury of the Queen

Though revered as the guardian of marriage and family, Hera's name was equally feared, invoked with awe for the divine vengeance she brought upon those who defied her order. Her fury, thunderous and unrelenting, was not born of spite but of devotional duty. To betray the vows she sanctified was to awaken a goddess who defended her throne, her dignity, and the eternal laws of fidelity. In her fury, legends were forged—tales that shaped the moral fabric of gods and mortals alike.

When Zeus strayed, it was not only he who bore the cost. His lovers and their children became symbols of defiance in Hera's eyes—living reminders of broken vows and callous insult. Her punishments were swift, her reach unrelenting. Yet they were not acts of blind cruelty, but justice—acts of preservation for the sacred bonds she was sworn to uphold. Her revenge became a spiritual correction, ensuring that the institution of marriage was not mocked without consequence.

Hera's justice extended beyond her personal wounds. She struck down hubris wherever it rose. In the tale of Ixion, a mortal king who dared to lust after the queen of the gods, Hera laid a trap—a phantom crafted in her likeness. When his offense was revealed, Zeus cast Ixion into eternal punishment, bound to a flaming wheel that spun forever through the shadows of the underworld. Hera's role was not merely reactionary—it was the spark of divine reckoning.

Through every tale of vengeance, Hera emerged as a goddess of iron will and unwavering purpose. Her fury was the flame that guarded sacred oaths; her punishments, the price of transgression. Yet this same force made her protector and avenger—a deity of boundless depth, where wrath and righteousness were one. In her dual nature—nurturer and punisher—she stood as one of the most formidable powers in the mythic world.

Through her unwavering defense of marriage, command over childbirth, and fearsome acts of justice, Hera's legacy endures as one of spiritual strength and venerated contradiction. Her myths, radiant with passion, turmoil, and devotion, continue to echo through time—reminders that love, loyalty, and power are never without trial.

CROWNED IN RITUAL AND WORSHIP

Hera's presence in Greek culture was deeply rooted in the values that shaped ancient life, reflected in festivals, rituals, and revered art. As protector of marriage, womanhood, and social order, she embodied moral authority and ethereal presence. The Heraia festival, held at Olympia, honored her through female athletic contests and rites that affirmed her role in civic unity and domestic strength. In myth and sculpture, she appeared as both nurturer and avenger—majestic, just, and unyielding. Through temples, stories, and ceremony, Hera endured not merely as queen of the gods, but as a symbol of Olympian law and mortal reverence.

> *"Queen Hera, the goddess who presides over marriage*
> *and protects the sanctity of the home,*
> *honored among the gods and mortals alike."*
> *— Hesiod, Theogony*

Games of Grace and Devotion

In the spiritual heart of ancient Greece, where the mortal world bowed to the divine, festivals honoring the gods shaped the rhythm of civic and spiritual life. Among them, the Heraia stood apart—a solemn and celebratory tribute to Hera, queen of Olympus and guardian of marriage and womanhood. Held at Olympia, beneath the gaze of her ancient temple, the festival marked Hera's revered place in society, especially among women who saw in her a model of strength, dignity, and heavenly guidance.

The Heraia's most distinctive feature was its athletic contests—footraces held every four years, not for men, but for maidens. With hair unbound and feet swift, young women raced in devotion, embodying discipline, purity, and the blessed transition from girlhood to womanhood. These events echoed the values Hera herself upheld: resilience, virtue, and the grace of purpose. Their movements across the stadium were not only sport, but sacred rite—a living hymn to the goddess who presided over life's most transformative thresholds.

Beyond the races, the festival was adorned with ritual and reverence. Worshippers brought finely woven garments as offerings, draping them upon Hera's statue within her temple—one of the oldest and most venerated in Greece. Sacrifices and prayers filled the air, each act a plea for protection, blessing, and the preservation of harmony within marriage and home. These devotions revealed the depth of Hera's cultural importance, and the profound respect she commanded among those who walked beneath her divine order.

Through the Heraia, Hera's myth stepped into civic life. The festival was not merely a celebration, but a declaration—of womanhood, fidelity, and spiritual unity. In honoring Hera, the women of Greece honored themselves, stepping forward in the public eye to affirm their place within a sacred tradition. Here, beneath the Doric columns and Olympian sky, Hera's legacy endured in footsteps, prayers, and offerings, eternal as the goddess herself.

Matron of Civil Harmony

Hera's power reached far beyond Olympus, into the very bones of Greek civilization. As the goddess of marriage, fidelity, and family, she stood as a mythic embodiment of order—guardian of vows, architect of harmony, and enforcer of spiritual law. Her myths do not portray her as passive consort, but as a force who fought to uphold the values on which both the heavens and mortal society depended. Her wrath, fierce and unrelenting, was not aimless—it was a fire lit in defense of promises once sworn.

Again and again, Hera defended the sanctity of marriage against betrayal and deceit. Those who dared undermine its sacred bonds faced her divine retribution. To the Greeks, her vengeance was not cruelty but justice—an affirmation that commitments were revered and not to be cast aside. Her punishments were acts of restoration, realigning what pride or passion had disrupted, and reasserting the authority of the moral order.

Her influence rippled through the polis as well. Hera was more than a guardian of homes—she was a sentinel of society itself. Her bond to the Furies, avengers of broken oaths and crimes against nature, echoed her commitment to justice. She ensured that covenants were kept, duties honored, and that the social fabric did not fray under the weight of human failing. In her, the Greeks saw not only heavenly power, but the reflection of their highest civic ideals.

Within the halls of Olympus, Hera's role was no less vital. She stood not only as queen but as mediator, guiding immortal quarrels toward balance, even when wounded by Zeus's betrayals. Her trials mirrored the burdens of leadership—bound by pride, yet called to preserve unity. Through these tales, Hera emerged not as a figure of fragility, but as a symbol of strength tempered by responsibility and wisdom.

In Hera, the Greeks found more than myth—they found a mirror of their world. Her presence infused the mortal sphere with dedicated expectation: that loyalty would be honored, justice upheld, and tradition revered. Through her, the divine law became mortal practice, and the struggles of Olympus became the guideposts of human life.

Marble, Gold, and Glory

The majesty of Hera was not confined to myth alone—it echoed through marble, pigment, and architecture, where her image was sculpted with reverence and awe. Greek artists sought to capture the duality that defined her: the serene queen and the storm-bound avenger, the radiant matron and the unyielding enforcer of celestial order. In each medium, Hera emerged as a symbol of regal grace and unshakable power.

In sculpture, she was most often depicted enthroned, a goddess of poise and sovereignty. Her form conveyed serenity, but her posture radiated command. A scepter in her hand marked her rule; a pomegranate, her bond to life, fertility, and the eternal cycle. Crowning her brow, the golden diadem signaled her unmatched status among the Olympians, casting her in the image of the numinous mother and queen.

Vase paintings and reliefs told the stories that shaped her legend. Scenes of her marriage to Zeus—moments of divine union and cosmic balance—were rendered in flowing robes and graceful gestures. These images idealized not only her beauty but her role as the embodiment of marital ideals: poised, proud, and dignified.

Symbols sacred to Hera adorned her likeness. The peacock, its feathers radiant with the eyes of Argus, often accompanied her—a testament to her vigilance and splendor. The cow, gentle and maternal, underscored her role as a nurturer, a protector of families, and a spiritual matron of life's quiet strength.

In stone and column, her temples stood as living monuments. The Heraion at Samos and the great sanctuary at Argos rose in her honor—structures of immense scale and reverent detail. Their friezes and carvings whispered her myths into stone, offering worshippers not only places of devotion, but sanctified spaces where art and divinity met.

Through these works, Hera's legacy was etched into the cultural memory of Greece. Artists captured her not just as a goddess, but as an eternal presence—her beauty exalted, her justice honored, her sovereignty preserved in form and color. In every figure, every temple, every painted line, the queen of Olympus reigned still.

CROWN OF WRATH AND GRACE

Hera, sovereign of Olympus and keeper of sacred vows, stands as an enduring symbol of loyalty, justice, and Olympian resolve. Her myths reveal a goddess of profound contradiction—nurturing yet relentless, regal yet wrathful, a guardian of harmony and a force of divine reckoning. As protector of marriage and family, she upheld the bonds that shaped both mortal lives and celestial order. Her fury, far from petty, was the fire of pride wounded, of vows broken, of sanctity defied.

From her tempestuous union with Zeus to her unyielding pursuit of justice, Hera's influence shaped the fate of gods and mortals alike. Her spirit lived in festivals and temples, in the prayers of brides and the cautionary tales of the unfaithful. Through the Heraia, her image was honored; through art and ritual, her legacy was sealed. She did not ask for reverence—she demanded it, and in doing so, became an immortal emblem of love's strength and power's burden.

As we depart from the realm of the queen, we descend from Olympus into the vast, churning dominion of another mighty god. Poseidon, lord of the sea, rules not with law but with force—his moods as shifting as the tides he commands. In the next chapter, we will journey into the deep, where ancient monsters stir, islands rise, and the god of oceans leaves his mark on myth and memory alike.

CHAPTER 4

POSEIDON

God of the Sea

Poseidon's legend surges like the tides he commands—vast, restless, and charged with Olympian might. Born of Cronus and Rhea, he rose with Zeus and Hades to carve the cosmos into realms of sky, sea, and shadow. To Poseidon fell the dominion of the deep, a kingdom as fierce and fathomless as the god himself. His myths sweep through ancient shores and sunken cities—from the lost glory of Atlantis to the shaping of Medusa's curse, and the bitter contest with Athena over Athens. In every tale, he is both maelstrom and builder, destroyer and giver of life. Poseidon is the ocean's living will—a force of creation entwined with wrath, whose stories echo the eternal struggle between chaos and order, power and restraint.

> *"Poseidon, who shakes the earth and commands the restless waves, his trident a symbol of unbridled power over the seas and storms."*
> — *Homer, The Iliad*

Division of the Cosmos

In the wake of the Titanomachy, as the old order crumbled beneath Olympian thunder, three brothers stood upon the precipice of a new world—Zeus, Poseidon, and Hades. With the Titans vanquished and Olympus ascendant, they turned to the solemn rite of dividing the universe, not by decree, but by lot—entrusting their fates to chance, or perhaps to the hidden will of fate herself.

To Zeus fell the vault of the heavens, crowned in celestial storm and sovereignty. Hades descended to the underworld, a realm cloaked in shadow where the souls of the dead wandered in silence. Poseidon, drawn to the endless rhythm of tides and tempests, claimed the sea—its depths boundless, its moods as mercurial as the god who ruled them. His trident cleaved the waves and stirred the tides, and his domain surged with power both creative and catastrophic.

Yet Poseidon's dominion was no mere watery exile. He was Earthshaker, sculptor of coastlines, father of horses, and harbinger of quakes. His realm teemed with mystery and momentum, a living embodiment of freedom and fury. It whispered promises of beauty and vengeance, calm and chaos.

Though balance had been struck, the brotherly accord bore beneath it a quiet tension. The sea, the sky, and the underworld would forever pull against one another, and Poseidon—proud, relentless, and mighty—would not suffer obscurity. His ambitions rippled through celestial halls and mortal realms alike, a reminder that even among gods, dominion is never without contest.

Rise and Fall of Atlantis

Among the deepest echoes of Poseidon's legend lies the tale of Atlantis—an island kingdom born from mythic love and buried beneath divine judgment. As recounted by Plato, the sea god was enraptured by a mortal woman named Cleito. On a sacred hill crowned by springs and fertile groves, Poseidon encircled her home with alternating rings of earth and sea, a symbol of both protection and power. From their union emerged ten sons, and upon them Poseidon bestowed a gleaming empire, each prince entrusted with a portion of the land that flourished under their father's favor.

Atlantis was a realm of marvels. Its citadels gleamed with orichalcum, its temples soared skyward, and its people lived amid abundance and sacred rites. With Poseidon's blessing, the Atlanteans prospered—builders of wonders, guardians of wisdom, and stewards of sacred gifts. Yet, as the generations passed, their hearts grew heavy with pride. Piety gave way to ambition, and the Atlanteans reached beyond their shores, seeking dominion over distant lands and defying the gods themselves. Even a kingdom born of love could not withstand the weight of mortal pride.

Poseidon's gaze, once warm with affection, turned cold with fury. The sea, his eternal ally, surged against its former children. The earth quaked, the skies darkened, and Atlantis—jewel of the deep—was swallowed whole by the ocean. Its towers collapsed beneath the tide, its memory reduced to myth, its legacy a warning etched in the silence beneath the swells. Thus, what was born of love was claimed by wrath, and Poseidon's gift became a grave. The tale of Atlantis endures as a haunting reminder of the cost of hubris—and the peril of a god betrayed.

Curse of the Gorgon

Equally potent and tragic is the myth of Medusa—a tale not of nations, but of a single soul caught in the torrent of Olympian desire. Medusa, once a radiant maiden and a devoted priestess of Athena, became the object of Poseidon's longing. In the shadowed stillness of Athena's sacred temple, the sea god pursued his passion and claimed Medusa upon ground consecrated to chastity and wisdom. The act, whether seen as violation or conquest, ruptured the sanctity of the divine, and punishment soon followed—but not upon the god who transgressed.

Athena, incensed by the desecration of her shrine, turned her wrath upon the mortal victim. Medusa's golden hair became a nest of living serpents, her eyes cursed with a gaze that turned all it met into stone. Where once there had been beauty, there now stood terror. Cast out from the world of mortals and gods alike, Medusa wandered the edges of myth, a symbol of horror—yet behind her monstrous visage lay a tale of unjust punishment, heavenly indifference, and the cruel weight of fate.

Though Poseidon remained unscathed, Medusa bore the scars of a crime committed in a god's passion and a goddess's pride. Her transformation reflected the imbalances of Olympus, where power often eclipsed justice. She became a legend of both dread and pity—a mirror to divine caprice and mortal suffering. Through her, Poseidon's legacy was stained with sorrow, revealing the harsh dualities of his character: creator and destroyer, lover and despoiler, a god whose desires could ignite both awe and anguish.

Strength or Wisdom

Among the immortal rivalries etched in mythic lore, none shines brighter than the fateful contest between Poseidon and Athena for the soul of a rising city—Athens. It was a clash not merely of gods, but of visions: one rooted in might, the other in wisdom. Atop the sacred heights of the Acropolis, the immortals gathered to witness which deity would bestow the greater gift and, in doing so, claim the city's eternal devotion.

Poseidon, god of the boundless sea, stood first. Striking the stone with his trident, he summoned forth a roaring spring of saltwater—a symbol of his power, his dominion over oceans, and the strength he offered to a warrior city. His gift surged with energy, wild and untamed, a promise of conquest and maritime glory.

Then came Athena, goddess of wisdom and craft. She knelt and touched the earth, and from that quiet gesture rose the olive tree—modest in appearance, yet rich in meaning. It offered wood for shelter, oil for light and nourishment, and fruit for sustenance. Her gift spoke of peace, prosperity, and endurance—the slow, patient victories of civilization.

The gods, moved by the olive tree's enduring value, awarded the city to Athena. Thus Athens bore her name and her spirit, a beacon of reason in a world often ruled by force. But Poseidon, wounded in pride, struck back. He unleashed torrents and upheaval upon the land, not out of petty rage, but from the depths of a god who could create beauty or ruin with equal force. His fury drenched the fields and battered the shores, a reminder that even in defeat, the sea would not be silenced.

This myth echoed far beyond the Acropolis. It was a tale of dualities—strength against wisdom, the elemental against the cultivated, the transient surge of power against the lasting roots of growth. Though Athens honored Athena as its protector, Poseidon remained venerated, his name whispered in the winds and etched in the tides.

Through his rivalry with Athena, Poseidon revealed his essence: not simply the god of the sea, but the embodiment of primal might and divine pride. His myths shimmer with contradiction and consequence, illuminating the restless depths of the god who forever shaped the fate of land and sea alike.

TIDES OF HEAVENLY POWER

Poseidon's powers surged from the raw essence of nature—vast, volatile, and divine. As lord of the seas, he ruled the tides and storms, his trident capable of summoning tempests or calming the surge. Earthquakes answered his fury, and mountains trembled at his command. Yet he was not only a god of destruction. From seafoam, he created the horse, a creature of speed and grace, and fathered beasts that roamed both land and ocean. His dominion extended beyond the deep, shaping land, sea, and myth alike. In Poseidon, beauty and terror moved as one.

> *"He roused the waves of the deep and*
> *called forth the storms,*
> *Poseidon, the earth-shaker,*
> *whose trident can split the*
> *mountains and churn the seas."*
> *— Homer, The Odyssey*

Sea and Quaking Earth

Poseidon's dominion over the oceans was as boundless as the seas themselves. From his coral and gem-encrusted palace beneath the thunder of the breaking surf, he commanded the waters with sacred authority—summoning crashing torrents or stilling the tides with a flick of his trident. The waves answered his will, and the winds bowed before him. To mortals, he was both a savior and a threat, capable of delivering safe passage or sending ships to their doom.

Sailors revered Poseidon with trembling respect, knowing that the calmest voyage could turn deadly if the sea god grew restless. It was custom to offer tributes before departing—coins cast into the surf or animals sacrificed on the shore—tokens of humility before a god whose favor could not be taken for granted. Poseidon's temperament mirrored the sea itself: changeable, vast, and unforgiving.

His power extended beyond the ocean's edge. As the Earthshaker, Poseidon ruled over earthquakes, splitting the earth with a single strike. Entire cities could be reduced to rubble when his fury was provoked. These were not merely natural tremors but god-forged proclamations—warnings from the god who governed both the restless waters and the trembling land beneath.

A vivid example of Poseidon's wrath lies in the epic journey of Odysseus. After the hero blinded Polyphemus, Poseidon's son, the god of the seas unleashed storm after storm, scattering the crew and prolonging Odysseus's return. The seas became a battleground, each wave a trial of endurance. In this myth, Poseidon's might shines through—creator of roiling surge, shaker of earth, and eternal force of awe, fury, and transformation.

Spawn of Seafoam

Poseidon's powers of creation rivaled the fury of his storms. Among his most wondrous acts was the birth of the horse—a creature forged from seafoam and immortal will. As myth tells, Poseidon shaped the first horse from the restless surf, gifting it the strength of ocean surges and the grace of wind-driven tides. Their gallop mirrored the sea's rhythm, swift and fluid, as if the very spirit of the water coursed through their limbs.

Yet horses were but one marvel of his mythic artistry. The oceans, Poseidon's realm, teemed with beings born of his imagination—creatures both enchanting and fearsome. Most iconic among them were the hippocamps: sea horses with equine torsos and fish-like tails, who drew the god's chariot across the deep. They symbolized his sovereignty over land and sea, blending terrestrial majesty with marine mystery.

But Poseidon's creations also reflected his darker moods. When angered, he summoned monsters to enforce his will. One tale tells of a colossal sea serpent sent to ravage Troy after its people defied the gods. Such creatures, born of Olympian rage, served as living warnings—proof that Poseidon's power was not limited to beauty and bounty but extended to terror and divine consequences.

Wrath and Consequences

Poseidon's temper, vast as the seas he ruled, was a force few dared provoke. Though capable of great generosity, his anger could rise as swiftly as a tidal rage, releasing waves of his vengeance to sweep away cities, kings, and even gods. His fury, unbound and elemental, mirrored the ocean's mood—serene one moment, cataclysmic the next.

In the great saga of the Trojan War, Poseidon's hand moved both subtly and with fury. As the Greek fleet gathered at Aulis, a dead calm stalled their sails. Though attributed to Artemis's displeasure, the Greeks saw in the sea's silence the shadow of Poseidon's might—a numinous force waiting to be appeased. Later, when the Greeks offered their cunning wooden horse, the Trojan priest Laocoön warned of treachery. But Poseidon, favoring the Greeks, sent sea serpents to silence him and his sons, ensuring the horse would breach Troy's gates. Thus, the god of seas also became the architect of the city's fall.

Another tale of profound retribution unfolds in Crete. King Minos, who vowed to sacrifice a sacred bull to Poseidon, broke his oath. In retribution, the god cursed Minos's wife, Pasiphaë, with a monstrous passion. From this union came the Minotaur—a beast of shame and punishment, housed in a labyrinth built to conceal the sin and appease the gods. Here, Poseidon's wrath did not crash like a wave but spread like a curse, reshaping destiny itself.

His rage was also etched into the earth. During the Gigantomachy, Poseidon pursued the giant Polybotes across the Aegean. Seizing a fragment of the island Kos, he hurled it with thunderous force, burying the giant beneath what would become Nisyros. In one mythic act, landscape and legend were fused, the isle a lasting scar from the god's righteous rage.

Yet Poseidon's wrath, though terrible, was not senseless. It bore the weight of justice and the expectation of reverence. His earthquakes and storms were divine reminders—lessons in humility, signals that mortals tread in a world governed by powers beyond their reach. To the ancient Greeks, Poseidon was not merely a sea god. He was a force of cosmic balance—creator and destroyer, protector and punisher—whose moods shaped myth, molded nations, and reminded all who sailed or ruled that the will of the gods was as deep and unfathomable as the sea.

ECHOES OF THE SEA

Poseidon's presence surged through the heart of Greek culture, anchored in towering temples like the Isthmian Sanctuary, infused in maritime rituals, and immortalized in epic verse. His worship reflected the reverence of a people bound to the sea, who saw in him both guardian and tempest. Through sacred festivals and coastal rites, he stood as the heavenly force behind safe passage and sudden peril. In myth and poetry, Poseidon embodied the sea's eternal tension—life-giving and ruinous—ensuring his legacy endured as a god of boundless power, mystery, and elemental majesty.

> *"Poseidon, the earth-shaker,*
> *who stirs the sea with his trident,*
> *and whose power no man or god may defy."*
> — *Homer, The Iliad*

Sanctuaries of Stone and Salt

In the sacred geography of ancient Greece, where earth met sea in eternal embrace, the reverence for Poseidon took form in stone and ritual. Chief among his sanctuaries stood the Isthmian Sanctuary, poised near Corinth on the slender land bridge that bound the Peloponnesus to the mainland. Flanked by the ceaseless waters he commanded, this hallowed site rose as a living tribute to the god who ruled with trident and tidal surge.

Here, the tides of faith surged. Pilgrims, sailors, and merchants gathered to offer prayers, libations, and sacrifices, seeking safe journeys and favor upon the seas. The temple itself, with columns rising like ocean swells, echoed Poseidon's might—its architecture a hymn of stone to his boundless dominion. Every carving, every offering, was a gesture of awe before a god who stirred both storm and serenity.

The sanctuary was not merely a place of worship—it was a crucible of culture and glory. Every two years, the Isthmian Games drew the faithful to honor Poseidon through chariot races, footraces, music, and solemn rites. Victors, crowned with wreaths of pine, were seen as chosen by the god himself, their triumphs not just physical feats but sacred affirmations of favor.

This sanctuary stood as more than a monument—it embodied the soul of a people bound to the sea. It reflected the divine intersection of commerce and culture, of power and piety. Within its bounds, Poseidon's presence surged like the tide, shaping not just the coastline, but the very spirit of Greek civilization.

Guardian of Shores and Sailors

To the ancient Greeks who dwelled along the restless coasts and sailed the vast Aegean, Poseidon reigned not only as a god but as the unseen captain of every voyage. His dominion over the sea marked him as both guardian and adversary—his favor a shield, his wrath a maelstrom. In a world where the ocean gave life and threatened to take it away, Poseidon was worshipped with awe and dread in equal measure.

For mariners, Poseidon was the arbiter of fate. Before embarking, sailors poured wine into the waves, cast offerings into the deep, and whispered prayers beneath wind-stirred skies. These rites were acts of devotion and survival, seeking calm tides and safe harbors. The sea's temperament mirrored Poseidon's own—placid one moment, raging the next. A sudden squall was no mere shift in weather but a sign that the god had turned his gaze—and perhaps his fury—upon the vessel.

Along the shorelines, entire communities placed their fortunes in Poseidon's hands. Fishermen entrusted him with the bounty of the deep, while merchants and port cities depended on his grace to secure trade and shelter. When earthquakes shattered the earth or waves rose without warning, it was said the Earthshaker had stirred. In response, offerings multiplied, and temples filled with supplicants seeking to calm the god whose trident could sunder land and sea alike.

Yet Poseidon's presence was more than elemental force. He symbolized the sea's dual nature: its bounty and its peril, its mystery and its might. His trident stood as a sacred emblem of that power, capable of drawing forth springs, raising islands, or destroying cities in a single strike.

Cities born of salt and wind—Corinth, Athens, Rhodes—held Poseidon in highest regard, their prosperity tied to his favor. His temples towered over harbors, silent sentinels to a god whose reach extended from the depths of the sea to the souls of those who dared navigate it. Through Poseidon, the Greeks saw not only the sea's vastness but its soul—and they honored it in the god who ruled its ever-changing face.

In the Songs of Heroes

Poseidon's presence surges through the tide of Greek epic literature, not merely as a deity, but as an Olympian force whose moods steer the fate of heroes and the rise and fall of kingdoms. In these ancient texts, his power is not confined to the sea—it becomes a narrative tide, sweeping mortals into trials shaped by vengeance, justice, and transformation.

In Homer's *Odyssey*, Poseidon emerges as a relentless adversary. When Odysseus blinds Polyphemus—the god's wrath coils like an untamed storm. The tranquil path home becomes a voyage of suffering. Waves crash, winds howl, and islands vanish on the horizon as Poseidon hounds the hero across the sea. Yet his fury is not wanton. It is purposeful, forging Odysseus into something more than a warrior: a leader tempered by hardship, humility, and resolve. In this way, Poseidon becomes both obstacle and teacher, an agent of mythic transformation.

In the *Iliad*, Poseidon's role shifts from punisher to strategist. Initially an ally of the Greeks, he withdraws his favor when pride blinds them to the sacred laws. His shifting allegiances remind readers that the gods are not passive overseers but volatile powers whose personal grievances shape the tide of war. His presence looms behind every surge in battle, a silent force tilting the balance of victory and ruin.

Elsewhere, in Hesiod's *Theogony*, Poseidon stands among the elder Olympians, a pillar of cosmic order with dominion drawn at the dawn of time. Later dramatists and poets would invoke him again and again—not only as the Earthshaker and Stormbringer, but as a symbol of scared duality: creator of wonders and unleasher of doom.

These epic portrayals reveal a god at once majestic and mercurial, feared yet venerated. Through Poseidon, the Greeks explored themes of immortal justice, mortal pride, and the fragile line between survival and destruction. In the vast ocean of myth, his voice crashes like thunder, and his will—etched in wave and word—shapes the destiny of heroes and the soul of a civilization.

THE SEA REMEMBERS

Poseidon, sovereign of the sea and shaker of the earth, stood as a symbol of elemental majesty—his domain vast, his moods as shifting as the tides. Wielding his trident, he could calm the waves or shatter mountains, his will etched into the waters that lapped every shore. Through the division of the cosmos, the rise and fall of Atlantis, and his tempestuous rivalry with Athena, Poseidon's reach stretched from the ocean's depths to the hearts of cities and kings.

Yet his essence flowed deeper than rage and conquest. He was the father of sea-beasts and sky-borne stallions, the silent guardian of sailors, and the ethereal artisan who shaped life from foam and fury. His nature mirrored the sea itself—unpredictable, breathtaking, and profound—a force to be worshipped, appeased, and understood.

As the tide of Poseidon's myths recedes, we set foot upon fertile soil and follow the path of another power—Demeter, goddess of grain and grief. In the chapter ahead, we journey into fields golden with harvest and shadowed by sorrow, where the rhythms of life and death are sown in sacred rites and remembered in the turning of the seasons.

CHAPTER 5

DEMETER

Goddess of Agriculture and Fertility

Demeter's tale is one of sacred sorrow and renewal. When Hades seized her daughter Persephone, the earth withered under the goddess's grief. In her wandering, she bestowed the Eleusinian Mysteries upon humankind—rituals veiled in death, rebirth, and spiritual truth. From her anguish sprang the seasons, mirroring the descent and return of her child. Her myth endures as a symbol of nature's rhythm, the power of maternal love, and the balance between life's bounty and its loss.

> *"Demeter, giver of rich gifts, the bringer of seasons,*
> *who nurtures the earth with life-giving bounty."*
> — *Homeric Hymn to Demeter*

Descent of the Maiden

Demeter's story begins with a bond as sacred as the soil she blessed—a mother's fierce devotion to her only daughter. Persephone, radiant with the vitality of spring, was her joy and pride, a living emblem of innocence and natural beauty. As goddess of agriculture and fertility, Demeter nourished all life, but none was dearer to her than the child who embodied the bloom of the earth itself.

This harmony was violently broken when Hades, ruler of the underworld, beheld Persephone and desired her as his queen. One day, as she wandered through a sunlit meadow gathering wildflowers, the earth groaned and split. From the chasm rose Hades in his obsidian chariot, cloaked in shadow. He seized her in silence and vanished into the abyss below. Her cries pierced the air, yet only Helios—the all-seeing sun—witnessed the abduction.

Demeter, unaware of her daughter's fate, wandered the earth in sorrow. For nine days and nights, she ate nothing, rested not at all, and called Persephone's name into a sky that offered no answer. Her anguish cast a chill over the land, and the fields withered under her grief. On the tenth day, Helios revealed the truth: Hades had taken Persephone, and Zeus had given his consent. Heartbroken and enraged, Demeter abandoned Olympus. Clothed in mortal form, she withdrew from the world of gods and vowed that the earth would bear no fruit until her daughter was returned.

As famine spread and the mortal world languished, Demeter came to Eleusis. There, among humble people, she revealed her immortal nature and taught the sacred rites that would become the Eleusinian Mysteries. These rituals, shrouded in secrecy, offered insight into life, death, and the promise of rebirth, reflecting the goddess's own journey through despair and renewal.

Through this myth, the sorrow of Demeter and the descent of Persephone became the eternal rhythm of the seasons—the withering fall and barren winter, followed by spring's triumphant return. More than a tale of loss, it is a sacred rhythm of death and life, a heavenly assurance that even in the darkest depths, reunion and renewal await.

Seasons Born of Grief and Return

Demeter's grief for Persephone did not remain her own—it rippled across the cosmos, unraveling the harmony between heaven and earth. In her sorrow, the goddess withdrew her blessing from the soil. Her grief cast a shadow across the fields, turning abundance to absence, fertility to famine. Verdant fields faded to ash, trees cast off their leaves like mourning garments, and cold silence gripped the land. The earth, once a cradle of life, became a barren echo of Demeter's broken heart—frozen, joyless, and incapable of renewal.

Far below, in the shadowed halls of the underworld, Persephone longed for the light she had lost. Though Hades treated her with reverence, she remained a captive queen—her radiance dimmed, her spirit veiled by the gloom. As famine spread and the cries of mortals reached Olympus, the gods pleaded with Zeus. Disturbed by the ruin of the world and the fate of his creations, the king of gods at last commanded Hades to release her.

The lord of the dead consented—but not without guile. Before Persephone departed, he placed in her hand a pomegranate, rich with crimson seeds. She ate of it, unaware that this simple act bound her to his realm forever. When mother and daughter were at last reunited, their embrace stirred the earth to bloom—but joy mingled with sorrow. For Persephone, having tasted the fruit of the dead, could not remain above eternally. She was now a creature of two worlds.

Thus a celestial bargain was struck. Persephone would dwell part of the year with Hades and part with Demeter. And so the seasons were born. When Persephone returned to her mother, Demeter's joy awakened the world—spring unfurled, summer ripened. But when her daughter descended once more into shadow, the goddess's grief spread across the land—autumn withered, winter fell silent. This sacred cycle, carved into the turning of the year, became a reflection of life and death, presence and absence, descent and return.

In this myth, the ancient Greeks found meaning not only for the changing earth but for the aching heart. Demeter's tale became a symbol of eternal rhythms—grief tempered by hope, loss softened by reunion—an enduring promise that all things lost may one day rise again.

Blessings and Wrath

Among the immortals, Demeter stood apart—not remote nor aloof, but intimately bound to the fate of humankind. As the goddess of agriculture, she sustained mortal life itself, her gifts of grain and cultivation shaping the very foundation of civilization. Through her blessings, the fields bore fruit, and the people flourished. Yet her bond with mortals was not without conditions. She could be both guardian and avenger, embodying the sacred balance between abundance and retribution.

When she wandered in mortal guise to Eleusis, weary from grief, she found shelter in the house of King Celeus. Cloaked in humility, she was welcomed with kindness by his household. Moved by their hospitality, Demeter sought to repay them with a mythic favor. She began a sacred ritual to render the infant prince, Demophon, immortal—anointing him by night and placing him within the sacred hearth to purge his mortal frailty through flame. But the ritual was broken. The child's mother, overcome with fear, interrupted the rite, and the blessing was left undone.

Though the boy's immortality was lost, Demeter did not curse the house. Instead, she unveiled her immortal form and, in a gesture of eternal generosity, entrusted the people of Eleusis with the Eleusinian Mysteries—rites of profound secrecy that bridged mortal life with celestial understanding. Through them, she offered not only sustenance for the body, but awakening for the soul.

Yet those who defied her sanctity tasted her wrath. In one tale, the arrogant Erysichthon dared to cut down a sacred grove consecrated to the goddess. Enraged by this sacrilege, Demeter laid upon him a terrible curse—unceasing hunger. No matter how much he devoured, his craving deepened. His wealth vanished, his body wasted, and at last, driven to madness, he consumed even that which should never be touched. His fate stood as a grim warning: to violate the sanctity of nature was to court ruin.

Demeter's dealings with mortals revealed the fullness of her divine nature. She was a nurturer and a judge, a provider of life and its guardian. Through her myths, the Greeks came to revere the earth not only as a source of sustenance, but as a sacred trust—to be honored with reverence, gratitude, and restraint.

GIFTS OF EARTH AND SPIRIT

Demeter's powers embodied the sacred rhythm of life—governing the fertility of the earth, the turning of the seasons, and the mysteries of death and rebirth. Through her grace, fields flourished and harvests sustained humanity. Her sorrow brought famine; her joy awakened the land. Honored in the Eleusinian Mysteries, she bridged mortal and immortal, offering not just sustenance but spiritual truth. Demeter's presence reminded all that nature's gifts required reverence, and through her, the Greeks understood the sequence of loss, renewal, and the enduring soul of the earth.

> *"Demeter, who brings forth the fruitful harvest,*
> *whose hands cradle the earth's bounty,*
> *and whose voice calls forth the seasons."*
> — *Homeric Hymn to Demeter*

Fertility and the Sacred Rhythm

Demeter's dominion over the earth's fertility and the sacred rhythm of agriculture made her one of the most vital and revered deities in the Greek pantheon. Her presence stirred in every golden field, every orchard heavy with fruit, every vine swelling with promise. To the ancient Greeks, Demeter was not merely the guardian of the harvest—she was its living soul. Her spiritual essence permeated the soil, calling forth life from the dust and sustaining the world with her harvest.

The power to awaken the land was both her gift and her burden, one she bore with reverent care. She governed the seasons, determining when the earth would bloom and when it would slumber. Her influence guided every stage of the harvest—from the casting of seeds into furrowed earth to the reaping of ripened grain. Farmers invoked her name before plow met soil, and the first sheaves of wheat were laid upon her altars in gratitude and awe. Without her blessing, the rains withheld, the fields grew barren, and famine stalked the land.

Through her mastery of growth and decay, Demeter embodied the fragile harmony of life on earth. Her power was a sacred covenant—offering sustenance while demanding humility. In her myth, the Greeks found more than a patron of crops; they found a mythic reminder that prosperity was born of balance, that the fruits of the earth required not just labor, but reverence.

Life, Death, and Rebirth

Demeter's power reached far beyond furrows and fields—she governed not only the growth of grain, but the hidden truths of existence itself. Through her mythic sorrow and sacred rites, she became a divine bridge between the living and the dead, shaping Greek understanding of life's impermanence and the soul's return. Her grief as a mother, mourning Persephone's descent into the underworld, formed the spiritual heart of her myth and deepened her place in the cosmos.

Persephone's abduction and return stood as a sacred allegory. When Hades drew her into the underworld, Demeter's mourning stilled the earth, ushering in winter's stillness—a season where life withdrew into silence. Yet with Persephone's return, warmth stirred, flowers awakened, and the land rejoiced. This rotation of descent and emergence echoed nature's eternal rhythm, casting the seasons as a reflection of divine loss and reunion, death and rebirth.

Demeter's influence extended into the afterlife through the Eleusinian Mysteries, rites veiled in secrecy yet rich with promise. Those initiated into her sacred tradition believed they glimpsed the path of the soul beyond death—an understanding not of finality, but of transformation. In Demeter's worship, the fear of death was softened by the hope of renewal, and the mortal spirit found communion with the heavens.

Through her sacred grief and celestial revelation, Demeter came to symbolize the great cycle that binds all things. She was the earth's heartbeat, the womb and the tomb, the presence that whispered to mortals that even in darkness, life waits to rise again. In honoring her, the Greeks found comfort in impermanence and faith in return—each season, each ending, a prelude to awakening.

Sacred Rites for Harvest

Demeter's powers were not only honored—they were invoked through sacred rites woven into the very fabric of Greek life. These ceremonies transcended simple devotion; they were acts of communion between mortals and the gods, expressions of reverence for the earth's abundance and the goddess who made it possible. In every furrowed field and every grain-laden altar, Demeter's presence was called forth to awaken life from the soil.

Foremost among these rites was the Thesmophoria, a solemn and mysterious festival observed by women across Greece. Over three sacred days, participants enacted rituals steeped in symbolism—death, decay, and renewal. Sacrificial offerings, often pig remains and other organic matter, were buried in the earth to decay. Days later, these remains were unearthed and mixed with seeds, becoming a powerful symbol of fertility reborn from dissolution. Through this act, the Greeks honored the sacred truth that life springs from death, and nourishment from sacrifice.

Beyond such grand rites, Demeter was honored in countless local traditions. Farmers offered the first fruits of their harvest to her altars in gestures of gratitude and hope. Communities held processions, sang hymns, and prepared feasts in her name—celebrations not only of plenty, but of the sacred contract between humanity and nature. These rites acknowledged that the gifts of the earth came not by chance, but by heavenly favor—and that favor demanded humility, reverence, and reciprocity.

Demeter's rituals were both practical and profound. They reminded the Greeks that agriculture was not merely labor, but sacred partnership—a balance of human effort and immortal will. Through these ceremonies, Demeter's essence was invoked not just in temples but in every planted field and every shared meal.

Her dominion spanned fertility, harvest, life, and death. Yet it was through these sacred rites that her presence became most immediate—a goddess of sustenance and transformation, linking the turning of seasons to the turning of souls. In her story, the Greeks found more than myth—they found meaning in the earth's rhythms, and hope in the eternal return of life.

RITUAL, MEMORY, AND MYTH

Demeter's presence shaped Greek culture through sacred festivals, revered temples, and enduring symbols that honored her role as life-giver and spiritual nurturer. Her power was invoked in rites of fertility and renewal, while altars and sanctuaries stood amid fields she blessed. Symbols like wheat, the cornucopia, and the narcissus echoed her gifts, linking earth's abundance to heavenly grace. Through her myth, the Greeks found meaning in the changing seasons, and in Demeter's sorrow and joy, they saw reflected the eternal bond between humanity, nature, and the sacred forces that governed both.

> *"Fair-haired Demeter, whose fruit the earth bears,*
> *and whose gift is the blessed grain that nourishes all*
> *mankind."*
> — *Hesiod, Theogony*

Secrets in Life and Afterlife

In the sacred heart of Greece, where gods walked among mortals in myth and memory, the worship of Demeter endured as one of the most profound religious traditions. Foremost among these was the Eleusinian Mysteries—ancient rites cloaked in secrecy and steeped in reverence. Held each year in Eleusis, these ceremonies honored the ethereal bond between Demeter and Persephone, transforming myth into a spiritual passage from loss to renewal.

The Mysteries echoed the tale of Persephone's descent and Demeter's mourning. Initiates—pilgrims of all ranks—underwent rites of purification before entering the Telesterion, a great hall where the sacred drama unfolded. Bound by oath, they never revealed what was shown, but it was believed that the Mysteries unveiled truths of the afterlife, offering hope, transformation, and the promise of rebirth.

These rites were not separate from the land—they were born of it. As Demeter's sorrow withered the earth and her joy restored its bloom, the Mysteries celebrated the eternal cycle of death and life, winter and spring. Open to all who sought divine understanding, the ceremony united Greeks across city and class, forging a common reverence for the forces that governed both nature and soul.

Beyond Eleusis, other festivals honored Demeter's gifts. The Thesmophoria, a sacred rite held by women, celebrated fertility and the mysteries of renewal. Over three days, they enacted rituals of burial and decay, returning offerings to the earth to awaken its life-giving power. This rite not only honored Demeter but reflected the essential role of women as guardians of life and sustenance.

Through these festivals, the Greeks did more than worship—they participated in the sacred rhythms of the world. In Demeter's name, they honored the fields, the family, and the fate of the soul, weaving her myth into the seasons of both earth and spirit. Her mysteries endured not in words, but in the circle they sanctified—in every seed buried, every harvest reaped, and every mortal who dared hope that death, too, was but a doorway to return.

Sanctuaries of the Earth Goddess

The worship of Demeter left a sacred imprint upon the landscape of ancient Greece, etched in temples and altars that rose like prayers from the earth she blessed. These hallowed sites, often nestled among fertile plains or bordering golden fields of wheat and barley, stood as sanctuaries of devotion and lifeblood for the communities they served.

Foremost among them was the Sanctuary at Eleusis, the beating heart of Demeter's cult. There, the Telesterion—the great initiation hall—welcomed pilgrims from across the Greek world. Within its vast, echoing walls, mortals crossed a threshold into the divine, participating in the Eleusinian Mysteries beneath ceilings carved with reverence. The architecture itself spoke of awe, built to hold the sacred and the seeking alike.

Beyond Eleusis, her temples dotted the land and reached across the sea. In Sicily, whose soil was rich with life, Demeter's worship flourished. The city of Enna, believed to lie near the very meadow where Persephone vanished into the underworld, became a sacred center of remembrance. Altars rose in her name, draped with offerings—grain, fruit, garlands—symbols of life entrusted to the goddess who governed its return.

These sanctuaries were more than places of worship—they were touchstones of survival and gratitude. Before the first seed touched the soil, farmers made offerings at her altars, seeking the goddess's blessing for rains, sun, and yield. During festivals, these spaces came alive with sacred processions, hymns, and feasts, binding mortals in shared reverence for the divine force that fed them.

Demeter's altars, though often modest, carried immense spiritual weight. Wreathed in wheat and adorned with fresh blossoms, they reflected her essence—nurturing, enduring, close to the earth. Each act of devotion was a covenant, a gesture of humility before the one who could summon life from the furrow or let it fall to ruin.

Through these temples and altars, Demeter's presence lived not only in myth but in stone and soil, in the rhythms of planting and reaping. They stood as testaments to a goddess whose power sustained the body and sanctified the land—forever entwining divinity with the everyday life of Greece.

Symbols of Sustenance and Power

Demeter's immortal essence was rendered not only in myth but in sacred symbols—emblems that captured her power, her grace, and her eternal bond with the living earth. Chief among these was wheat, the golden grain that fed the body and echoed the cycles of life. To the ancient Greeks, wheat was not merely sustenance—it was Demeter's blessing made visible, a sacred thread between goddess and mortal.

In art and sculpture, Demeter often appeared crowned with grain or bearing a sheaf of wheat in her arms, embodying the promise of the harvest. Each seed planted mirrored her myth: the descent into darkness, the wait in silence, and the triumphant return. The act of harvesting became a ritual reenactment of rebirth, a tribute to the goddess whose sorrow once stilled the land and whose joy restored its bloom. Wheat adorned her altars, was woven into her festivals, and stood as a constant reminder of her sustaining hand.

The cornucopia, the horn of plenty, was another potent symbol—an overflowing vessel of fruits, grains, and flowers, it signified the boundless generosity of Demeter's gifts. Appearing in frescoes, statuary, and coinage, the cornucopia celebrated abundance and the earth's reward for reverence. It became a visual hymn to her providence, a symbol of peace born through nourishment.

Among the most poignant of her symbols was the narcissus— a flower tied to the beginning of her sorrow. It was this bloom that lured Persephone to the meadow, where Hades rose from the depths to claim her. The narcissus came to represent beauty touched by tragedy, and the eternal balance between life's joy and its inevitable loss. In Demeter's rites, the flower was more than decoration—it was remembrance.

Through wheat, the cornucopia, and the narcissus, the Greeks honored Demeter not only as a goddess of grain, but as a spiritual force whose presence shaped the seasons, the soil, and the soul. These sacred symbols served as daily devotions—tangible echoes of a myth that bound heaven to earth, and humanity to the ever-turning wheel of life and renewal.

THE SOIL SPEAKS HER NAME

Demeter's story is etched into the soil and soul of the ancient world—a tale of love and sorrow, of absence and return. Her devotion to Persephone, and the anguish that followed their separation, gave birth to the seasons themselves, casting the natural world in the image of a mother's grief and joy. Through this sacred myth, the Greeks came to understand the eternal rhythms of life, death, and rebirth that governed both the earth and the soul.

As the goddess of agriculture, Demeter bestowed not just sustenance but knowledge—teaching mortals how to till, to sow, to reap, and to honor the land that sustained them. Yet hers was not a gentle dominion alone. When her gifts were defiled, her wrath was swift and sacred. Her myths remind us that abundance is not given freely—it is earned through reverence, reciprocity, and harmony with the god-forged order. Even the gods, bound by the laws of nature, could not escape her fury.

Demeter's legacy lived on in the rites and festivals that bore her name. The Eleusinian Mysteries, veiled in silence and wonder, offered initiates a glimpse into the secrets of the afterlife, promising hope beyond the grave and a bond with the gods that transcended death.

And now, from Demeter's fertile domain, we turn toward a different form of power—one born not of soil and seed, but of intellect, justice, and war. Athena, goddess of wisdom and battle, awaits us. In the next chapter, we shall witness her miraculous birth, her guardianship of cities and heroes, and the strategic brilliance that made her a cornerstone of Olympus. Where Demeter nurtured life, Athena shapes its destiny.

CHAPTER 6

ATHENA

Goddess of Wisdom and War

Born in a flash of divine intellect from Zeus's brow, Athena emerged fully armed—a goddess of wisdom, warcraft, and reason. Her myths weave tales of balance and clarity: the judgment of Arachne, the contest for Athens, the calm strategist amid divine tumult. As guardian of heroes, she shaped the fates of Odysseus and Perseus, guiding them with unseen strength. In every tale, Athena stands as the radiant force of intellect and justice—unyielding, measured, and revered—her presence etched into the very soul of Greek myth.

> *"Athena, bright-eyed and wise, whose counsel brings victory, and whose hand wields the spear with the strength of gods."*
> — *Homer, The Iliad*

Born of Thought and Thunder

Athena's origin is among the most astonishing in all of Greek myth—fitting for a goddess born of pure intellect and divine strategy. Her emergence was unlike any other: a tale where wisdom, might, and fate converged in one resounding act of creation.

It began with Zeus, sovereign of the gods, who sought to guard his reign from the threat of prophecy. When warned that his child with Metis, goddess of wisdom, might one day surpass him, Zeus acted with ruthless foresight. He swallowed Metis whole, believing her knowledge could be absorbed, her power subdued. Yet within him, Metis already carried a child destined for greatness.

As time passed, Zeus was seized by a tormenting pain—an unbearable pressure that thundered within his skull. In desperation, he called upon Hephaestus, Olympian smith and craftsman. With a single mighty stroke of his hammer, Hephaestus split open the god-king's brow, and from the wound leapt Athena—fully grown, armored in radiant bronze. Her piercing cry shook the heavens, a herald of celestial purpose and unmatched resolve.

Her birth, forged not in flesh but in thought, marked her as a singular force—born of mind, not womb; of vision, not impulse. She emerged as both warrior and guardian, intellect clad in armor, wielding truth as her shield and reason as her spear. From that moment, the pantheon stood transformed, for Athena had arrived—not merely as a goddess, but as the very embodiment of clarity, justice, and immortal thought.

Weave of Hubris and Mercy

Among Athena's many legends, the tale of Arachne stands as a solemn parable—one that threads together pride, artistry, and heavenly judgment. Arachne, a mortal of rare talent, became renowned throughout Greece for her mastery of the loom. Her tapestries shimmered with life, and her fame grew until she dared proclaim her skill superior to that of Athena, patroness of weaving and wisdom itself.

Disguised as an old woman, Athena approached the boastful weaver and urged her to show humility. But Arachne, blinded by arrogance, rejected the warning. The goddess then cast off her disguise and challenged the mortal to a contest of craft. Both set to work, and what followed was a duel not of weapons, but of thread and vision. Athena wove scenes exalting the gods, full of harmony and divine majesty. Arachne, bold and defiant, depicted the gods' failings—tales of deception and folly rendered with stunning precision.

Though Arachne's artistry rivaled the divine, her insolence could not be forgiven. In a torrent of fury, Athena destroyed the tapestry and struck the mortal down. But when Arachne, stricken with shame, sought death, the goddess relented. In a gesture of both mercy and punishment, she transformed her into a spider, granting her the eternal task of weaving. Thus, Arachne's legacy endures—forever crafting, forever bound to the lesson that skill without reverence invites ruin.

Olive and Ocean

Another tale of lasting power is the divine contest between Athena and Poseidon for the patronage of a city yet to be named. When the people sought a guardian among the gods, both deities stepped forth to claim the honor. To settle the matter, each would offer a sacred gift, and the people would choose whose boon best served their future.

Poseidon, the Earthshaker, struck the earth with his trident, and from the wound surged a saltwater spring—mighty and brimming with spectacle, yet barren to the taste. Athena answered with quiet strength. Kneeling, she planted the olive tree, whose branches bore fruit, oil, and wood—symbols of peace, sustenance, and enduring prosperity.

The citizens, discerning the true value of the gifts, chose Athena. Enraged, Poseidon unleashed his wrath, flooding parts of the land. But Athena stood resolute, her foresight undiminished by his fury. From that day forth, the olive tree became the living emblem of the city, and its name—Athens—echoed her triumph. In this contest, the gods themselves bore witness to a truth eternal: that thoughtful foresight triumphs over brute force, and that the gifts of vision root deeper than the tides of wrath.

Protector of Heroes

In the realm of gods and mortals, Athena stood apart—not as a bringer of chaos or capricious fate, but as a spiritual architect of justice and strategy. Where others acted from passion or pride, her aid was measured, her purpose clear. To the heroes of ancient Greece, she was not merely a benefactor but a guiding force— bestowing insight, courage, and the tools of triumph upon those deemed worthy.

Among her most favored was Odysseus, the cunning king of Ithaca. In the pages of Homer's *Odyssey*, it is Athena who steers him through the storm of trials following Troy's fall. She shields him in disguise, lends him counsel in moments of peril, and pleads with the gods for his safe return. Her favor is not blind—it is earned, drawn to the brilliance of Odysseus's mind, which mirrors her own: sharp, adaptable, and resolute.

Perseus, too, rose to greatness beneath her gaze. Tasked with slaying Medusa—a creature whose very eyes turned men to stone—he turned to Athena for aid. She offered him a polished bronze shield, a mirror of survival, through which he viewed the Gorgon without meeting her deadly stare. Guided by her strategy and protected by her gifts, Perseus struck true and reshaped his destiny.

Even Heracles, lion-hearted and thunder-strong, was not beyond Athena's reach. In the Labor of the Stymphalian Birds, brute strength proved useless against a sky swarmed with shrieking death. It was Athena who armed him with a tool of heavenly invention, proving that might alone cannot silence chaos—only the marriage of wisdom and force can prevail.

Athena's guardianship of heroes was no mere divine whim; it reflected the sacred ideals of Greek heroism: intellect in concert with courage, discipline joined with daring. She bestowed her favor not upon the boldest, but upon the most virtuous, the most clever, the most just. Through them, her spirit moved—shaping the fates of mortals, inspiring the myths that echo across time, and proving that true greatness begins in the mind.

BALANCE OF MIND AND MIGHT

Athena's powers reflect a sacred balance of intellect, creativity, and discipline—marking her not as a force of fury, but as the embodiment of purpose and wisdom. In war, she stands as a master strategist, favoring precision over bloodlust, guiding battles with calm calculation rather than chaos. Her strength lies not in brute force, but in the clarity of thought and the art of timing. Beyond the clash of arms, Athena is the divine patron of crafts, invention, and reason. She inspires artisans, architects, and lawmakers alike, elevating civilization through innovation and order. As a mediator, she tempers conflict with justice, ensuring that vision—not wrath—prevails.

> *"Athena, who with wisdom and strength,*
> *guides the minds of men and gods,*
> *her spear ever ready,*
> *her shield shining with justice."*
> *— Homer, The Iliad*

Warfare Woven in Wisdom

Among the Olympians, Athena stood apart as the embodiment of war refined by clarity—a goddess who wielded intellect with the same precision as spear and shield. Unlike Ares, who reveled in the chaos and bloodlust of battle, Athena governed the disciplined art of warfare: order amid tumult, strategy over savagery. Her presence on the field was not the storm, but the calm that commands it—her mind a fortress of foresight.

Athena was no frenzied combatant; she was a tactician, a mythic general clad in gleaming armor, crowned with the aegis—the fearsome goatskin bearing the petrifying gaze of Medusa. Yet her true power lay not in weapon or ward, but in the clarity of vision that could unravel any enemy's plan. In the *Iliad*, she guided heroes like Diomedes and Odysseus, lending courage and cunning in equal measure. When Diomedes stood against Ares himself, it was Athena's hand that steadied his aim, proving that mortal will, shaped by divine wisdom, could challenge even gods.

Her greatest stratagem came not by sword, but by subterfuge: the Trojan Horse, a gift of guile that brought mighty Troy to ruin. It was Athena who inspired the plan, seeing what others could not—how patience, deception, and long-sighted design could achieve what brute force could not breach. For her, victory was not destruction for its own sake, but the restoration of balance and the forging of peace through reasoned triumph.

In Athena, the Greeks saw the perfect warrior—not driven by rage, but by justice; not hungry for conquest, but devoted to purpose. She was war's intellect, its soul disciplined, its fury bound by thought.

Mistress of Knowledge and Craft

Athena's power flowed far beyond the din of battle, touching the mind, the hand, and the soul. As goddess of wisdom and invention, she was the sacred muse of philosophers, artisans, and all who sought to shape the world through thought and craft. Her birth—emerging full-formed and armored from the mind of Zeus—was a living symbol of intellect made divine. Yet her wisdom was not cloistered in abstraction; it was living, breathing, practical. She taught mortals to tame the soil, fashion tools, and weave beauty from thread—laying the very foundations of civilization.

Her patronage of crafts was etched in the myth of Arachne, the mortal who dared rival the goddess in weaving. Though Arachne's skill was real, her pride defied the divine. Athena's response, part punishment and part mercy, transformed her into a spider—forever weaving, forever remembering. This tale revealed Athena's reverence for mastery tempered by humility, and the sacred origins of human ingenuity.

Beyond the loom and plow, Athena presided over law, reason, and the soul of the city. In Athens, her chosen domain, the heights of philosophy, art, and governance bore her mark. Leaders looked to her for clarity; builders and thinkers honored her in every design. Through her, mortals were gifted not only with knowledge, but with the power to create, to question, and to elevate. In every solved problem and crafted wonder, Athena's spirit endures—a goddess who shaped the mind of Greece and defined the essence of human progress.

Voice of Reason, Hand of Justice

Though Athena bore the spear and shield, she was no warmonger. She stood not only as a goddess of war, but as a guardian of order—a divine arbiter who sought peace through wisdom and resolution over wrath and ruin. Where other deities thrived on turmoil, Athena wielded reason as her mightiest weapon, her presence in conflict marked by clarity, justice, and a tireless pursuit of balance.

In the vast saga of the Trojan War, her actions were not born of vengeance, but of principle. She championed the Greeks not from favoritism, but because Paris, in choosing Aphrodite over her, had scorned the values she embodied—wisdom, honor, and rightful judgment. Even amid the clash of blades and cries of war, Athena's hand guided her champions to fight with discipline and dignity, her influence a force that shaped conduct as much as conquest.

Her role as mediator was not confined to mortal wars. In one tale, when Poseidon and Zeus stood poised on the brink of Olympian strife, Athena's voice of reason stilled the storm. Through measured counsel and deft diplomacy, she dissolved their conflict before it could fracture Olympus, proving that the strongest gods listened to the wisest words.

Yet it was in the trial of Orestes that Athena's legacy as a peacemaker became eternal. Pursued by the Furies for the murder of his mother, Orestes faced numinous judgment. Athena, presiding over the trial, introduced the jury—a sacred birth of law—and cast the deciding vote that freed him. In that moment, vengeance gave way to justice, and a new order rose: one governed by reason, not rage.

Athena's gift to mortals was not peace without struggle, but the path to it—marked by insight, tempered by fairness, and sealed by law. In courts, councils, and quiet decisions, her spirit lingers still—the voice that calms the storm, the mind that heals the blade.

In Stone and Celebration

Athena's presence shaped the heart of Greek civilization, especially in Athens, the city that bore her name. The Parthenon stood as a sacred tribute to her wisdom and strength, while her symbols—the owl and olive tree—embodied knowledge and peace. Celebrated through grand festivals like the Panathenaia, Athena united the people in reverence and civic pride. More than a deity, she was a guiding force in law, learning, and democracy. Her influence transcended myth, becoming the soul of a culture where intellect governed action and justice bore the voice of the divine.

> *"Athena, whose wisdom and valor*
> *guide the hands of artisans*
> *and the hearts of warriors, revered*
> *in temples and honored in the arts."*
> — *Hesiod, Theogony*

Sacred Temple and Devotion

In the heart of ancient Athens, crowning the heights of the Acropolis, stood the Parthenon—a monument not merely of worship, but of wonder. Dedicated to Athena Parthenos, the Virgin Goddess, it rose as a testament to the city's devotion, a fusion of divine reverence and mortal brilliance. Its towering columns and sculpted friezes proclaimed Athens as a beacon of intellect, power, and piety, guided by the hand of its patron goddess.

Within the temple stood a statue of Athena as awe-inspiring as the edifice itself. Fashioned by the master sculptor Phidias, it gleamed in gold and ivory—Athena, fully armored, bearing the goddess Nike in one hand, while at her feet rested a great shield adorned with scenes of mythic triumph. This image embodied her dual nature: warrior and sage, protector and patron of civilization's rise.

Athena's bond with the city was also honored in grand festivals that stirred the heart of Athens to celebration and unity. Foremost among them was the Panathenaic Festival, held every four years— a sacred convergence of faith, art, and athleticism. A great procession ascended the Acropolis, bearing a newly woven peplos to adorn her image, while the city rejoiced with music, poetry, contests, and games. These events reflected all that Athena championed: strength in body, brilliance in mind, and harmony in spirit.

Through the enduring grandeur of the Parthenon and the unifying power of her festivals, Athena's spirit became inseparable from the identity of Athens itself—a goddess woven into the very fabric of its glory.

Vision in Feathers and Branch

Athena's divine essence found form in symbols that spoke to her wisdom, strength, and harmony with the natural world. Chief among these were the owl and the olive tree—sacred emblems that echoed her presence across temples, coins, and hearts.

The owl, sharp-eyed and silent, often perched upon Athena's shoulder, symbolized perception beyond illusion. A creature of the night, it could see what others could not—into shadow, into truth. To the Greeks, it became the living image of insight and foresight, reflecting Athena's gift of strategy and discernment. So closely tied was this bird to her ethos that its likeness adorned Athenian coinage, a mark of divine intellect guarding the city's fortune.

The olive tree, her enduring gift to Athens, stood as a symbol of peace, prosperity, and sacred utility. Where Poseidon summoned a stormy spring, Athena planted a tree—offering nourishment, oil, and shelter to her people. Its fruit lit their homes, fed their bodies, and anointed their rituals. Through this gift, Athena claimed the city not through force, but through foresight made manifest in the everyday lives of its citizens.

These symbols transcended myth, becoming threads in the fabric of Greek culture. In every grove and every painted amphora, in silver drachmas and carved stone, the owl and the olive tree whispered of Athena's watchful gaze. They bound mortal and immortal, reminding all that the goddess of wisdom walked among them—not in thunder, but in thought, sustenance, and enduring vision.

Voice of Law and Civic Reason

Athena's presence was not confined to temples or mythic tales—she dwelled in the very heart of Athens's political life, shaping the ideals that gave rise to one of history's greatest experiments in governance. As the goddess of wisdom and strategy, she embodied reason, balance, and justice—virtues that formed the bedrock of Athenian democracy.

Under her divine gaze, Athens grew into a city-state where discourse held more sway than conquest. The olive tree she gifted—offering peace, prosperity, and sustenance—became a living emblem of civic harmony. Her favor was seen not as distant blessing, but as direct guidance, her wisdom echoing through the voices of orators and the decisions of lawmakers.

In the democratic assembly, where citizens gathered to shape the fate of their polis, Athena's ideals prevailed. Debate, deliberation, and careful judgment reflected her nature as both strategist and mediator. Her influence was invoked in matters of war and reconciliation, in the forging of laws, and in the peaceful settlement of disputes—each decision a tribute to the goddess of thoughtful action.

Her role in the myth of Orestes further solidified her place as guardian of justice. By establishing the trial by jury and casting the final vote in favor of mercy, Athena replaced vengeance with law, chaos with order. This act enshrined fairness and due process as sacred principles—gifts not only to Athens, but to civilization itself.

Her wisdom reached into the city's soul, inspiring its schools, its temples, and its ideals. The pursuit of philosophy, art, and truth in Athens was more than cultural flourish—it was the legacy of Athena, alive in every enlightened mind and every just law. Through her, democracy was not merely a system—it was a sacred endeavor, a path lit by intellect and guided by the divine.

SHIELD AND SCROLL

Athena stands among the Olympians as a beacon of wisdom, strength, and deliberate power—a goddess whose presence brought order to chaos and reason to the passions of gods and mortals alike. Her myths reveal a divine protector who fought not with fury, but with purpose. She guided heroes such as Odysseus and Perseus, bestowed gifts that nurtured civilization, and shaped justice with a steady hand—ever balancing might with mind.

Her legacy lives on in the marble of the Parthenon, in the festivals that once stirred a city to reverence, and in the symbols that still speak of knowledge and insight. The owl, the olive tree, the aegis—all remind us of a goddess who ruled through intellect, discipline, and unshakable resolve. Athena proved that strategy could rival strength, and that clarity of thought was a force as enduring as any weapon.

Now, as we descend from the heights of her sacred temple, we turn our gaze to another radiant power of Olympus. In the next chapter, we enter the realm of Apollo—god of prophecy, healing, light, and song. There, we shall uncover the voice of the oracle, the harmony of the lyre, and the brilliance of a god whose influence reaches from mountaintop to mortal heart.

CHAPTER 7

APOLLO

God of the Sun and Arts

Apollo's legends form a radiant tapestry of power, prophecy, and passion, reflecting the divine paradox of brilliance and burden. Born beneath the sacred light of Delos, his arrival was heralded by awe and fear alike—a god destined to both heal and harm. With the slaying of Python, he claimed Delphi and sealed his place as the voice of eternal truth. Yet for all his celestial gifts— music, medicine, foresight—Apollo was no stranger to longing and loss. His myths shimmer with triumph and tenderness, revealing a god who illuminated the world with wisdom while walking the fragile line between glory and grief.

> *"Apollo, the far-shooter, whose silver bow sends arrows of plague and whose lyre brings the harmony of healing and art."*
> — *Homer, The Iliad*

Beneath the Palm

The birth of Apollo unfolds like a hymn of endurance and divine purpose—a tale marked by the exile of a mother and the rising of a god. Leto, the luminous Titaness graced with beauty and poise, drew the gaze of Zeus, and their union sparked the wrath of Hera, queen of Olympus. In jealous fury, Hera cursed Leto to wander the world, forbidding her sanctuary on any land touched by sun or bound to earth.

Across wind-lashed shores and distant mountains, Leto wandered in anguish, the weight of her unborn children growing heavy with fate. At last, she came upon Delos—a floating island untethered to sea or soil, untouched by Hera's cruel decree. There, amid the barren stones and salt-laced breeze, Delos offered refuge. In return, Leto vowed to bless the isle with divine favor, transforming it into hallowed ground.

Beneath the swaying branches of a sacred palm, to the song of waves and wind, Leto gave birth. First emerged Artemis, serene and swift, who turned and helped deliver her twin—a radiant child of prophecy and flame. As Apollo drew his first breath, golden light spilled across the island, and his cry echoed like a lyre strung with dawn. From that moment, the world knew a new god had risen— one born not merely of Olympus, but of struggle and splendor.

Delos, once rootless and forsaken, blossomed beneath Apollo's gaze. It became a beacon of pilgrimage and praise, a sacred shore where mortals came to honor the god of light, music, and oracles. Like the god himself, the island was transformed—proof that even in exile, greatness may be born.

Conquest of Python

In the early blaze of his divinity, Apollo faced a trial that would carve his name into the bedrock of destiny—the slaying of Python, the ancient serpent born of flood and shadow. Coiled around the sacred slopes of Mount Parnassus, Python guarded the chthonic oracle of Gaia, a vestige of the world before the Olympians. Its presence choked the land in dread, a symbol of primordial chaos resisting the dawn.

Still youthful but radiant with celestial purpose, Apollo beheld the beast and understood what must be done. This creature of rot and ruin stood between the old order and the light he was fated to bring. With bow in hand and divine fire coursing through his veins, he met Python in battle. The air thickened with venom and smoke, but Apollo's arrows flew swift and sure—each shaft a ray of clarity piercing through ancient fear.

When the serpent fell, writhing into silence, Delphi was transformed. No longer a place of terror, it became a sanctuary of prophecy. Yet even in triumph, Apollo honored the sacredness of his slain foe. To cleanse the act and consecrate the ground, he founded the Pythian Games—celebrations of strength and song, where mortals vied in athletic glory and poetic craft beneath the gaze of the god.

At Delphi's heart, Apollo raised his temple, crowned by the Oracle of Delphi. Through the trance-bound voice of the Pythia, his words reached kings, seekers, and heroes, echoing across ages as riddles of fate. Thus, through battle, reverence, and wisdom, Apollo claimed not only a sanctuary, but the soul of prophecy itself.

Love That Bloomed and Withered

Apollo's legacy, though radiant with prophecy and song, is etched equally in tales of longing, devotion, and sorrow. Though divine, his heart pulsed with mortal ache, and the passions he pursued wove a tapestry of beauty tinged with tragedy—revealing a god who could command the heavens yet falter before love.

Among the most haunting of his myths is that of Daphne, the forest nymph whose grace stirred Apollo's deepest desire. Struck by Eros's golden arrow, he burned with sudden infatuation, while Daphne, pierced by one that repelled affection, fled in terror from his approach. Through thickets and glades, she raced with desperation as Apollo pursued with relentless yearning. In her final plea, she called upon her father, the river god Peneus, who answered by transforming her into a laurel tree just as Apollo reached her.

Grief-struck yet reverent, Apollo embraced the tree, vowing that the laurel would be sacred in his honor—a living symbol of purity and unyielding will. Its leaves, ever green, would crown poets and victors, preserving Daphne's spirit in the wreaths of glory. In this tale of love unfulfilled, Apollo's passion was transfigured into tribute, and beauty found permanence in sorrow.

So too with Hyacinthus, the mortal youth whose radiance captivated the god. Bound by friendship and affection, the two competed in sport until a fatal discus—turned by the jealous wind god Zephyrus—struck Hyacinthus down. Apollo, overcome with anguish, could not heal the wound, and as the youth's life faded, he transformed his blood into the hyacinth, a flower blooming with the memory of love cut short.

Even the tale of Coronis bore bitter fruit. Though her betrayal kindled Apollo's wrath and sealed her fate, their union birthed Asclepius, god of medicine and healing. In him, Apollo's light found new form—not as song or vision, but as the power to mend what is broken. Thus, from sorrow rose salvation, and the line between punishment and providence blurred.

Through these stories, Apollo emerges not as a distant deity of perfection, but as a god intimately entwined with the mortal soul. His love stories—wrought with passion, jealousy, loss, and renewal—mirror the delicate threads of human emotion. From birth to battle, from longing to legacy, Apollo's myths reveal a divinity that shines not only with brilliance, but with depth, duality, and eternal resonance.

GIFTS OF THE SUN GOD

Apollo's powers radiate across the heavens and into the hearts of mortals, embodying the divine harmony of light, insight, and inspiration. As lord of the sun, he commanded the chariot of day, casting life and order across the earth with each golden arc. Yet his gifts extended far beyond the sky. In the arts of music, poetry, and healing, he moved with grace and mastery, a patron of beauty and balance. Most revered was his power of prophecy—voiced through the Oracle of Delphi—where his wisdom pierced the veil of fate, guiding mortals through shadow toward truth.

> *"Apollo, the far-shooter,*
> *whose golden lyre brings joy to the immortal gods,*
> *and whose arrows none may escape."*
> *— Homeric Hymn to Apollo*

Chariot of the Heavens

Among Apollo's most radiant powers was his dominion over the sun and its divine illumination—a mantle that crowned him as a god of life, truth, and celestial rhythm. Though the sun once belonged to Helios, it was Apollo who came to embody its enduring brilliance, not merely as a source of light, but as a force of order, revelation, and sacred balance.

Each dawn, legend tells, Apollo yoked his golden chariot to steeds of flame and rode across the heavens, his passage painting the sky in fire and glory. This daily journey was more than motion—it was the heartbeat of time, the cycle of birth and renewal, the god's blessing upon the world. Beneath his radiance, the earth awakened—crops flourished, shadows retreated, and the soul stirred with inspiration.

Yet the light of Apollo, like the sun itself, bore a double edge. Just as it warmed, it could sear. In moments of divine wrath, his arrows of light brought pestilence and ruin, unseen yet inescapable. Entire armies fell beneath their sting, struck by the hand of a god whose power was both healer and destroyer.

To the Greeks, Apollo's light transcended the physical. It was the light of the mind, the fire of clarity, the brilliance of truth breaking through illusion. His radiance did not simply reveal the world—it revealed the self, urging mortals toward wisdom, discipline, and the eternal pursuit of understanding.

Music, Verse, and Cure

Apollo's power resonated not only in light and prophecy but in the harmonies of sound, verse, and restoration. With his golden lyre—crafted by Hermes and strung with celestial grace—he became the divine embodiment of music and poetry, shaping chaos into beauty, discord into rhythm. Each note he plucked wove a thread of cosmic order, a melody capable of stirring the stars and steadying the soul.

The Muses, daughters of memory and keepers of inspiration, danced to his tune and sang beneath his guidance. As their leader and patron, Apollo infused mortal minds with the fire of creativity. Under his gaze, poets gave voice to the ineffable, and musicians channeled divine resonance through mortal hands. To call upon Apollo was to invite transcendence, to draw artistry from the breath of the gods.

Yet his influence stretched further—into the sacred art of healing. As the father of Asclepius, god of medicine, Apollo passed down the gift of restoration. He was invoked to cure, to purify, and to preserve the sacred balance between health and affliction. Whether guarding cities from plague or blessing physicians with insight, Apollo stood as a beacon of renewal.

His healing was not bound by flesh alone. Through music and poetry, he mended what pain silenced—soothing grief, awakening hope, and elevating hearts beyond despair. In this union of song and remedy, Apollo revealed a divine truth: that beauty heals, and healing is itself a form of art.

His patronage of the arts and the restorative spirit made him a god of harmony in every sense—a bringer of meaning, wonder, and light to the world of mortals.

Voice of Future

Among Apollo's many divine powers, none shone brighter in reverence and mystery than his gift of prophecy. As the god of oracles, Apollo bridged the realms of mortal uncertainty and divine foresight, offering glimpses into the threads of fate woven by the gods. His prophetic voice did not merely predict events—it guided kings, humbled heroes, and revealed the deeper truths buried beneath mortal desires and fears.

At the heart of this sacred power stood the Oracle of Delphi, nestled upon the sun-drenched slopes of Mount Parnassus. This ancient sanctuary, believed to be the omphalos—the navel of the world—was where heaven touched earth. Here, Apollo's radiant force was channeled through the Pythia, a mortal priestess who served as his mouthpiece. Seated above a fissure in the rock, inhaling vapors said to rise from the earth's soul, the Pythia entered a trance. In this ecstatic state, she spoke in cryptic phrases infused with Apollo's will, which temple priests then interpreted for seekers who came with questions weighty and wide.

These supplicants were not only poets and pilgrims but rulers and generals, each hoping to learn the gods' favor or the outcome of their endeavors. They asked whether empires would rise or fall, whether love would endure or falter, whether the paths they chose led to glory or ruin. The oracle's answers, though veiled in riddle and symbol, carried the authority of Olympus.

But Apollo's reach extended beyond Delphi. Shrines across the Hellenic world echoed with his insight. His counsel shaped laws, foretold omens, and often held mortals accountable for their choices. Yet his gift was not without shadow. In the tale of Cassandra, Apollo granted a mortal princess the power of true prophecy. When she spurned his love, he cursed her with disbelief—her visions doomed to be ignored. Thus, even truth could become torment.

Apollo's prophetic power was dual in nature—enlightenment entwined with challenge. To receive his guidance required not only reverence but discernment, for the path ahead was rarely straightforward. Through oracles, riddles, and divine signs, Apollo offered mortals the chance to glimpse destiny—not as a fixed decree, but as a mirror through which they might shape their future with wisdom, courage, and humility.

In this sacred gift, Apollo revealed not only what was to come but what one must become to face it.

ECHOES OF APOLLO

Apollo's influence permeated every facet of Greek culture, uniting prophecy, music, healing, and light into a single divine presence. As lord of Delphi, his oracle shaped the course of empires, while his lyre and laurel became enduring emblems of harmony and triumph. Through the healing arts of Asclepius and the inspiration of the Muses, Apollo elevated human creativity and knowledge. He was more than a deity—he was the guiding light of intellect and order, his legacy etched into temples, festivals, and the very spirit of a civilization that saw wisdom as divine.

> *"Apollo, master of the silver bow, who brings the light of wisdom and the harmony of the lyre to mortals and gods alike."*
> — *Homeric Hymn to Apollo*

Navel of the World

High upon the sacred slopes of Mount Parnassus, where earth's breath mingled with divine spirit, the Oracle of Delphi stood as a radiant pillar of Apollo's presence. This hallowed sanctuary, veiled in mystery and crowned in reverence, served not merely as a temple but as the very navel of the ancient world—a threshold where mortals approached the divine to seek wisdom forged beyond time.

Delphi's sanctity began with Apollo's triumph over Python, the ancient serpent who guarded Gaia's prophetic seat. With his bow of light, Apollo struck down the beast and sanctified the site in his name, transforming it into a realm of prophecy, clarity, and sacred utterance. Temples rose in his honor, their marbled halls gleaming with the tributes of kings, poets, and pilgrims who came bearing offerings for truth.

The Oracle, channeled through the Pythia—Apollo's chosen priestess—spoke in cryptic verse, her voice laced with divine fire. Seated above the chasm where earth's breath whispered secrets, she bridged the mortal and immortal realms, revealing destinies with words that shaped empires and altered fates. Her counsel, sought by the humble and mighty alike, was both gift and enigma—proof that even the gods favored those who sought wisdom over war.

Yet Delphi was more than a place of prophecy—it was a crucible of culture. The Pythian Games, held in Apollo's honor, exalted athletic might and artistic brilliance in equal measure, uniting body and mind in the sacred image of their patron. Music, poetry, and competition echoed through the valley, celebrating the god who illuminated both truth and beauty.

In every utterance of the Oracle, in every laurel crown bestowed, Apollo's essence endured. Delphi stood not just as a place—but as a testament to the god who brought order from chaos, light from shadow, and meaning from mystery. Through Delphi, Apollo became the conscience of Greece, his voice echoing across centuries as the golden standard of divine guidance.

Bringer of Harmony and Healing

Apollo's influence coursed through the very soul of Greek civilization, shaping its arts and healing practices with divine precision. As the god of music, poetry, and medicine, he bestowed upon mortals the sacred tools to elevate the spirit, soothe the body, and reveal eternal truths through inspired creation.

With his golden lyre, strung in perfect harmony, Apollo channeled celestial order into song. Each note sung by his hand was not mere music, but a hymn to cosmic balance. His melodies quelled storms, stirred hearts, and carried the weight of divine beauty. In leading the Muses—those radiant daughters of memory—Apollo inspired the flourishing of music, dance, and verse. Through their union, the arts became sacred rituals, honoring both mortal struggle and divine wonder.

Poets who invoked Apollo sought not just eloquence, but transcendence. Their words, guided by the god's unseen hand, painted the splendor of the natural world, the glory of heroes, and the mysteries of fate. Apollo lit the path for bards and storytellers, embedding wisdom in every line and revealing the divine spark within human expression.

Yet Apollo's gifts were not limited to the soul. He was also the healer who understood the delicate rhythms of the body and the shadow of affliction. He could summon plague with his arrows or dispel suffering with a touch. As father of Asclepius, the god of medicine, Apollo passed down sacred knowledge that became the foundation of healing across the Greek world.

Temples and sanctuaries rose in his honor, places where the sick sought divine intervention. In sacred sleep, offerings, and ritual, Apollo's presence was invoked to restore harmony. These centers of hope and restoration bore witness to the power of the divine to mend what was broken—not only flesh, but spirit.

Through the dual gifts of art and medicine, Apollo became the guardian of humanity's noblest pursuits. His power uplifted the soul, refined the mind, and mended the body. In every poem, in every cure, in every whispered prayer for inspiration or healing, his presence endured—an immortal guide through pain, beauty, and the endless pursuit of perfection.

Lyre of Harmony, Laurel of Victory

Among the sacred emblems of Olympus, none captured the essence of Apollo more fully than the lyre and the laurel wreath. These were not mere ornaments, but symbols of celestial purpose—each echoing the god's power to elevate, enlighten, and inspire.

The lyre, forged from a tortoise shell and gifted by the cunning Hermes, became Apollo's instrument of divine harmony. Under his touch, it sang with clarity and cosmic order, its chords binding heaven and earth in rhythm. Its music was no idle sound—it was the breath of beauty itself, capable of stirring nature to bloom, taming wild hearts, and restoring balance where there was discord. In Apollo's hands, the lyre became the voice of creation's symmetry, a testament to his dominion over both intellect and inspiration.

In sculpture and verse, the god is often shown crowned with radiance, his lyre beside him as the Muses dance in adoration. These daughters of memory followed his lead in art, song, and poetry, their every movement infused with the elegance of his melodies. To hear the lyre was to glimpse the perfection of the divine—a sound that awakened the soul and beckoned it toward higher truths.

Equally revered was the laurel wreath, born of sorrow and transfigured into glory. When Apollo's love for the nymph Daphne was denied, and she transformed into a laurel tree to escape his embrace, he did not curse her fate. Instead, he sanctified her form. The laurel would henceforth be his sacred tree, and its evergreen leaves a crown for those worthy of honor. Woven into wreaths, they adorned the brows of victors—poets, athletes, and leaders—who achieved greatness through discipline and grace.

But the laurel was more than a token of triumph. It symbolized purification and divine favor, a sign that the bearer had touched something eternal. In the rustle of its leaves, the Greeks heard the whisper of Apollo himself—reminding them that the path to excellence was paved with sacrifice, insight, and reverence for beauty.

Together, the lyre and laurel revealed the soul of Apollo. One sang of truth shaped into harmony; the other crowned those who rose to meet the divine within themselves. Through these symbols, Apollo's legacy endured—not just in myth, but in the living breath of culture, wisdom, and sacred aspiration.

ETERNAL RADIANCE

Apollo, the radiant son of Zeus and Leto, stood among the Olympians as a god of sublime contradictions—harbinger of light and shadow, harmony and retribution, prophecy and plague. His myths cast him as a primordial surge who illuminated both the path of truth and the price of hubris. From the sacred heights of Delphi, where his oracle spoke the will of the gods, to the echoing strings of his golden lyre, Apollo's presence shaped the very soul of Greek civilization.

He was a healer whose touch restored balance, yet also a wrathful deity whose arrows carried divine punishment. His pursuit of beauty—whether through love, art, or justice—was relentless, often blurring the lines between passion and consequence. In Apollo, the Greeks found not just a god of golden brilliance, but a mirror of their own dual nature: driven by reason, stirred by emotion, bound to fate yet reaching for the eternal.

His legacy endured in the harmony of music, the pursuit of knowledge, and the reverence for truth spoken through the veil of mystery. Apollo was the voice in the wind that stirred poets to verse, the light that guided kings toward wisdom, and the flame of intellect that dispelled darkness from the human soul. He was Apollo—bringer of vision, punisher of pride, the golden god who stood at the meeting point of fire and form, voice and vengeance.

Now, as we leave behind the gleam of Apollo's sunlit path, our journey turns to the moonlit wilds of Artemis. His twin sister, born beneath the same palm tree on Delos, walks a path of fierce independence and primal grace. In the next chapter, we follow the footsteps of the goddess of the hunt—guardian of nature, maiden of the silver bow, and protector of all who walk alone beneath the stars.

CHAPTER 8

ARTEMIS

Goddess of the Hunt and Wild Animals

The legends of Artemis resound with primal force and sovereign grace, revealing a goddess forged in wildness and bound by unyielding vows. Born in radiant harmony beside her twin, Apollo, she entered the world not as a child, but as a divine sentinel—sworn to eternal maidenhood and untouched by mortal desire. In the haunting tales of Actaeon and Orion, Artemis does not waver; she is both sanctuary and storm, a huntress whose arrows defend the sacred laws she alone enforces. Her mythos flows between nurture and fury, embodying the delicate symmetry of life sustained and limits enforced. In every grove and moonlit glade, she endures as the guardian of freedom and the fierce soul of the untamed.

> *"Artemis, the huntress, roams the*
> *wilderness with her silver bow,*
> *swift as the wind, her arrows true as the stars."*
> — *Homeric Hymn to Artemis*

Twin of the Sun God

Born beneath a sky shadowed by divine fury, Artemis emerged into legend alongside her twin, Apollo, in one of the most fateful births of the ancient world. Their mother, Leto—hunted by Hera's relentless vengeance—found no refuge until the floating isle of Delos welcomed her, untouched by curse and crowned with swaying palms. There, in the stillness of a sacred grove, Artemis came forth first—radiant, composed, and already cloaked in the dignity of divinity.

Yet her birth was no solitary triumph. In a moment steeped in wonder, the newborn Artemis turned to aid her suffering mother, guiding the arrival of Apollo with grace beyond mortal comprehension. Thus, their bond was sealed—not in play, but in purpose—an eternal union of light and shadow, sun and moon, god and goddess.

As Apollo rose to command the sun's brilliance, Artemis claimed the silver quiet of the moon. She became the spirit of the wilderness, of instinct and hidden paths, of independence untouched by rule. Together they formed the celestial balance— reason and intuition, clarity and mystery—but Artemis, ever elusive, walked a path of her own: a goddess of fierce grace, sworn to freedom, and forever bound to the untamed.

Oath of the Untouched Huntress

From the embers of her mother's suffering, Artemis forged a vow as resolute as moonlight upon stone—never would she bow to the bonds of love or the yoke of marriage. While still young, she swore to remain untouched by passion's chains, dedicating her soul to the wilderness, the sacred hunt, and the guardianship of the pure and unprotected. In this solemn oath, she defined her divinity— not through union, but through unyielding sovereignty.

Clad in silver and silence, Artemis gathered to her side a sacred band of nymphs—kindred spirits who shared her devotion to chastity and freedom. Together, they roamed through shadowed groves and mist-draped mountains, bound not by duty to others, but by their reverence for the untamed world. Hers was no cold heart, but one ablaze with purpose. Artemis did not flee love—she transcended it, choosing instead the exalted path of independence and command.

Yet in her fierce resolve, Artemis became more than a huntress—she was a guardian of life's fragile beginnings. Women in labor whispered her name through pain and prayer, trusting in the heavenly hands of a goddess who bore no child yet shielded every mother. She punished cruelty with merciless precision and uplifted the innocent with quiet strength.

Thus, her vow was no confinement but a crown—an emblem of celestial autonomy. Artemis stood apart, not in solitude but in supremacy, embodying both the feral majesty of nature and the unspoken grace that shelters the vulnerable beneath moonlit skies.

Hunted and the Hunter

The legends of Artemis blaze with purity and vengeance, revealing a goddess unshaken in purpose and sovereign in spirit. Nowhere is her divine nature more vividly etched than in the fates of Actaeon and Orion—two mortals who crossed her path, one by misstep, the other by bond, and whose stories echo with warning and wonder.

Actaeon, a master of the hunt, wandered unknowingly into sacred woods where Artemis and her nymphs bathed beneath veils of mist and moonlight. To behold the goddess unveiled was to trespass upon the holiest of sanctuaries. In that moment, Artemis did not hesitate. With a gesture born of wrath and sanctity, she transformed him into a stag—his form forsaken, his identity shattered. Hounded by his own loyal dogs, Actaeon perished, torn by the very beasts he once commanded. It was not cruelty but divine justice—swift and exacting—for the sanctity of Artemis's realm allowed no transgression, not even one unmeant.

Yet the tale of Orion casts Artemis in a different light, revealing the complexities that stir even within the heart of a maiden goddess. Orion, a towering hunter of immense skill, became her companion—equal in might, a kindred spirit beneath the stars. Together they chased the wild, bound not by desire, but by shared reverence for the freedom of the hunt.

But peace among immortals is seldom eternal. In some tellings, Apollo, wary of Artemis's growing closeness to Orion, devised a test cruel in its cunning. Pointing to a distant shadow in the sea, he challenged his sister to strike it with a single arrow—never revealing it was Orion swimming far below. Artemis, proud and unerring, loosed her shot. When the tide returned his lifeless form to shore, sorrow gripped her like no wound ever had.

To honor him, she raised Orion into the night sky, crafting a constellation of remembrance and regret. It was a celestial elegy, cast in stars, for a bond severed by deception and sealed by fate.

Together, the tales of Actaeon and Orion unveil the dual soul of Artemis—unyielding defender of sacred law and bearer of silent grief. She is the wild made divine, the moonlit protector who demands reverence, yet feels the ache of loss no less than mortals. In her myths live eternal truths: that freedom is a flame fiercely guarded, that love walks with risk even in its purest form, and that the gods, too, are shaped by sorrow and resolve.

BLESSINGS OF THE BOW

The powers of Artemis radiate with sacred balance, embodying both fierce autonomy and nurturing grace. As sovereign of the wild, she safeguards the natural world with unerring vigilance, maintaining the fragile harmony of forest and beast. Yet she is also the silent guardian of childbirth and protector of the young, offering strength in life's most vulnerable moments. Though untouched by mortal love, her compassion runs deep, expressed not in softness but in resolve. Her bow, ever flawless in aim, is both weapon and warning—a symbol of justice, independence, and divine precision. In Artemis, the wilderness finds its champion and the innocent their shield, united in the silent majesty of her eternal watch.

> *"And Artemis, with her golden arrows,*
> *strikes down the swift deer and roams the shadowy woods,*
> *mistress of the wild and the hunt."*
> — *Hesiod, Theogony*

Defender of the Wild

Artemis, goddess of the hunt, was the living spirit of nature's untamed majesty. Her presence stirred in the rustle of leaves, the cry of distant wolves, and the sacred stillness of ancient forests. Yet she was more than a huntress—she was the guardian of the wild, the vigilant steward of life's fragile equilibrium. Her dominion extended across the natural world, where she watched over beasts and glades with silent authority, ensuring that the wilderness remained unspoiled and sovereign.

In the shadowed depths of the forest, Artemis revealed the dual nature of the wild—its beauty and its brutality, its power to give and to take. She roamed freely with her loyal band of nymphs, protecting the creatures entrusted to her care. Deer, boars, and other sacred animals were not trophies, but charges under her mystical protection. When she hunted, it was with reverence, not cruelty. Each arrow served the hallowed balance, preventing the rise of chaos and preserving the harmony that allowed all life to flourish.

But her protection was not limited to animals—it extended to the land itself. Forests, mountains, and moonlit glades were consecrated by her presence, places where mortals were wise to tread lightly. Those who defiled these sanctuaries faced swift and merciless justice. In one such tale, King Oeneus neglected to honor Artemis during a harvest rite. In retribution, she summoned the Calydonian Boar, a monstrous beast that laid waste to his kingdom, a fated punishment for human arrogance.

Through her role as protector of nature, Artemis became a symbol of harmony and sacred order. She reminded mortals that the world was not theirs to conquer, but to respect. In her myths, the wild is not lawless—it is her realm, ruled by instinct, balance, and divine will. To live in peace with the earth, one must first honor the goddess who walks its hidden paths.

Mistress of Birth and Becoming

Though Artemis vowed never to wed nor bear children, she held an enduring and sacred bond with childbirth and the lives of women. This divine paradox was born of her origin—when, moments after her own birth, she aided her mother Leto in delivering her twin brother, Apollo. From this first act of grace and strength, Artemis emerged not only as huntress, but as a protector of those who labor to bring life into the world. In her, women found a fierce and compassionate guardian to whom they could pray for safe passage through the perils of birth.

As patroness of childbirth, Artemis embodied the quiet valor required to cross the threshold between life and death. Women called upon her name in their hour of need, invoking her courage to endure and her mercy to prevail. Temples raised in her honor became sanctuaries for expectant mothers—places where offerings were laid and prayers whispered with trembling hope. These consecrated spaces echoed with trust in her unseen presence, a divine ally amid the blood and breath of creation.

Her guardianship extended beyond the birthing bed to the rites of girlhood and growth. Artemis watched over young girls as they approached the sacred threshold of womanhood, guiding their steps through rituals that honored purity, strength, and transformation. Festivals in her name were woven with God-touched symbols of transition, where daughters of Greece took their first steps into adulthood under her watchful gaze.

Yet even in this nurturing role, Artemis remained inviolate—a goddess of fierce autonomy who walked alone beneath the moon. For Greek women, she stood as both nurturer and exemplar: the embodiment of strength, the keeper of feminine mysteries, and the divine promise that womanhood could be lived not only with devotion, but with defiance and freedom.

Bow of Silence, Strike of Judgement

Artemis's mastery of the bow was the stuff of legend—her arrows swift as moonlight, her aim guided by primordial instinct. No mortal and few gods could rival her precision, for in the hunt she became an elemental force: silent, graceful, and inexorably lethal. To witness Artemis in motion was to see nature's will embodied, her form flowing with the elegance of a river and the sudden strike of a storm. She was the wind through trees, the flash before death, the unseen power that governed the wild.

Her bow—silver or golden in ancient song—was a gift from Zeus, forged not as ornament but as extension of her indomitable will. It served as both shield and sword, a sacred tool through which she preserved balance and enforced sanctified justice. Whether felling sacred prey or striking down those who defied her laws, Artemis's arrows spoke with clarity—each one a verdict, final and unerring.

One such act of judgment came with the Calydonian Boar. When King Oeneus failed to honor Artemis during his harvest rites, she unleashed the monstrous beast upon his lands. A host of heroes, including the famed Atalanta, rose to the hunt—but Artemis's hand loomed over the chaos. Though she did not strike the boar herself, its very presence was her rage incarnate, a living reminder that to dishonor the goddess was to invite ruin.

Yet her arrows did not serve vengeance alone. Artemis, in her mercy, could grant the gift of a painless death. In moments of mortal agony, her arrows brought release—swift, silent, and free of suffering. Through this power, she held dominion over both ends of the mortal coil, as guardian of life and arbiter of death, uniting compassion with control.

Her unerring skill symbolized far more than martial prowess— it embodied her autonomy. While other gods wielded brute force or trickery, Artemis ruled through clarity and focus. She required no legion to defend her honor, no counsel to shape her path. In each shot, there lived her essence: resolute, sovereign, and free from sway.

In the bow of Artemis, the wild had a voice. Through her hunt, the heavens witnessed discipline shaped by instinct, and power wielded with sacred restraint. Her legacy—protector of life, enforcer of balance, patron of childbirth and mistress of the untamed—cements her as one of Olympus's most revered and complex deities. She stands forever at the threshold of nurture and ferocity, a goddess who evokes awe, demands respect, and inspires devotion.

HALLOWED PRESENCE IN HELLENIC LIFE

Artemis's presence in Greek culture was both vast and intimate—etched in the grandeur of temples and the quiet rituals of daily life. Sanctuaries like the Artemision stood in awe of her divinity, while rites such as the Brauronia honored her guidance through life's transitions. Her symbols—the silver moon and the sacred deer—embodied her dual essence as celestial huntress and earthly protector. Through consecrated architecture, ritual devotion, and enduring myth, Artemis became more than a goddess; she was a living presence in the Greek soul, a beacon of balance between wilderness and civilization, independence and nurture.

> *"Artemis, the maiden of the wild,*
> *whose silver bow brings swift deliverance,*
> *and whose dance stirs the leaves of the forest."*
> — Homer, The Iliad

Sanctuaries and Stone Shrines

The reverence for Artemis found its most enduring and awe-inspiring form in the grand sanctuaries raised in her honor, none more magnificent than the Artemision at Ephesus. Counted among the wonders of the ancient world, this temple stood as a tribute to the goddess's deified stature and the devotion she stirred in the hearts of her worshippers across generations.

Set within the thriving city of Ephesus, the Artemision rose in breathtaking splendor. Its towering columns and intricate reliefs reflected not just wealth or craftsmanship, but the mystic essence of Artemis herself—goddess of the hunt, guardian of the young, and protector of the natural order. Unlike sanctuaries that captured a single divine trait, the Artemision embraced her full nature: fierce and gentle, wild and wise.

Yet the temple was more than a place of prayer—it was a living center of culture and commerce. Pilgrims journeyed from distant lands to lay offerings at her altar, seeking favor, protection, or healing. Around its enshrined precincts, artisans, merchants, and citizens flourished, their daily lives enriched by the rhythms of worship. The Ephesia, a festival in her honor, blended solemn rite with artistic and athletic triumphs, reflecting Artemis's patronage of excellence and grace.

Though Ephesus housed her most renowned temple, Artemis was venerated in other hallowed places—at Brauron, where girls passed into womanhood under her watch, and at Delos, her birthplace, where the gods first met the world. These temples, nestled in nature's embrace, deepened her bond with the wilderness and the sacred spaces she vowed to protect.

Through these temples, Artemis's presence became stone and sanctuary. They were more than monuments—they were invocations of the divine, sanctuaries of balance and beauty where the goddess walked among mortals and left her eternal imprint on the soul of Greece.

Guide of Maidens and Mothers

Artemis's influence reached beyond temple walls into the most intimate moments of a woman's life, guiding her through the exalted thresholds of growth and change. As goddess of independence and protector of the innocent, Artemis presided over rites of passage that marked the journey from childhood to maturity. These rituals, often performed within her sanctuaries, were offerings of hope and reverence—calling upon the goddess to lend her strength to the unfolding path ahead.

Among the most renowned of these was the Brauronia, a festival held in her honor at Brauron. There, young girls approaching womanhood donned ritual garments and danced in sacred procession, embodying arktoi—bears sacred to Artemis. This symbolic transformation from girl to bear, innocence to strength, was more than performance—it was a spiritual metamorphosis, overseen by the goddess who stood at the edge of wildness and grace.

These rites served as sacred threads binding individual growth to the collective wisdom of the community. Artemis, ever watchful, stood as a beacon of protection, offering courage to those stepping into new roles. Her presence was both comfort and command, a reminder that strength dwells in every soul guided by purpose.

Even in the lives of brides and mothers—roles she herself rejected—Artemis remained near. Women prayed for her protection in childbirth, laid offerings at her altars, and invoked her name for safe passage through life's fiercest trials. Her paradoxical connection to these rites deepened her mystery: untouched by domestic ties, yet revered as a guardian of those who embraced them.

Through these ceremonies, Artemis became more than myth—she became a symbol of transformation. In her, women saw their own reflection: strong, evolving, and eternally tied to the rhythms of nature, independence, and becoming.

Crescent and the Wildlife

The symbols that defined Artemis's character echoed with special meaning, capturing the essence of a goddess who stood at the threshold of wildness and grace. Chief among them were the moon and the deer—sacred emblems that revealed her as both fierce huntress and silent guardian, radiant in mystery and resolute in protection.

The moon, with its ever-shifting phases, mirrored Artemis's connection to the natural world and its eternal rhythms. As a lunar goddess, she was the light that pierced the darkness, guiding travelers through shadowed paths and illuminating the wilderness with celestial calm. The moon's association with intuition, mystery, and quiet strength reflected Artemis's role as protector of the unseen and untamed—those who moved beyond the reach of ordinary sight.

In art and myth, she is often crowned with the crescent moon, a symbol of her sovereign dominion over night and sky. This luminous mark affirmed her bond with the divine feminine, her identity rooted in autonomy, cycles, and silent power. The waxing and waning moon became a living metaphor for her influence—embodying birth, growth, death, and rebirth—the sacred patterns that govern all life and reflect the goddess's enduring presence.

Equally vital was the deer, swift and elusive, a creature transcendent to Artemis since ancient times. The deer embodied the fragile beauty of nature, its grace intertwined with vulnerability, its survival dependent on divine protection. Artemis was often seen accompanied by these creatures, not as prey, but as companions— living testaments to her role as guardian of the wild.

One of her most sacred deer appeared in the myth of the Ceryneian Hind—a golden-horned creature so swift and mystical that only Heracles, charged with capturing it, dared give chase. For a full year he pursued it, until at last he stood before Artemis herself. Though she allowed him to fulfill his labor, it was only with her blessing, a reminder that even heroes must bow before the sacred symbols she claimed as her own.

Together, the moon and the deer reflect the full spirit of Artemis—untamed yet compassionate, remote yet deeply present. Through these symbols, she remained etched into the heart of Greek culture: a goddess who moved with the silence of moonlight and the grace of a fleeing stag, ever watchful, ever sovereign over the world she vowed to protect.

THE HUNT ENDURES

Artemis, fierce and free, stood as a radiant emblem of strength, purity, and heavenly resolve. As goddess of the hunt, guardian of the moon, and protector of women, she embodied the ancestral tension between compassion and wrath. Her myths reveal a deity as merciful as she was merciless—one who nurtured the innocent, defended the sacred, and struck down those who dared trespass her bounds. In Artemis, the Greeks saw the wild made divine, a sovereign spirit untouched by compromise and unbowed by the will of others.

Revered in temples and invoked in the hush of the forest, Artemis was a champion of women through every stage of life— especially in birth, growth, and transformation. Her rejection of marriage and her fierce autonomy set her apart from her Olympian kin, making her a symbol not only of chastity, but of freedom. She was bound to no one, beholden to none, and in that defiance, she inspired awe. Her sacred deer, her silver bow, and the moonlit trails she walked became timeless emblems of her dominion over the wild and the soul.

As we step away from her shadowed groves and silver-lit silence, we now enter a realm of fury and fire. In the next chapter, we turn to Ares—the relentless god of war. There, on blood-stained fields and amidst the clash of arms, we will uncover the myths of strife, conquest, and the volatile force that shaped both gods and mortals in the crucible of battle.

CHAPTER 9

ARES

God of War

The myths of Ares form a tempest of fury, pride, and divine contradiction. His bitter feud with Athena revealed the two faces of war—savage chaos against disciplined strategy. Yet in his fervent love for Aphrodite, a hidden tenderness stirred beneath the armor. On the bloodstained fields of Troy or amid the rivalries of Olympus, Ares surged forth as the raw, unrelenting spirit of battle. He embodied war's primal force—unyielding, unpredictable, and sublime—evoking both awe and sorrow in equal measure.

> *"Ares, insatiable in battle, whose joy is in the clash of arms, and whose strength is like the torrent of the war-god."*
> *— Homer, The Iliad*

Born for Battle, Bound by Rivalry

Ares, god of war and wrath, was born of Zeus and Hera—a union that forged not only a child, but a force of divine fury. From the moment of his birth, Ares carried the essence of unbridled conflict, a spirit untamed and steeped in blood. Unlike his sister Athena, who rose as the goddess of wisdom and the art of war, Ares surged with the primal energy of the battlefield—brutal, impetuous, and merciless. This sacred opposition carved the foundation of their eternal rivalry, setting mind against might within the courts of Olympus.

Where Athena inspired reverence through reason and restraint, Ares stirred dread through violence and fury. He charged into war with a wild heart and unthinking valor, blind to consequence, deaf to strategy. Athena, ever measured and composed, sought to impose order upon the chaos Ares unleashed. Their discord was no mere family feud, but a divine reflection of war's dual face—one side calculated and cold, the other savage and storm-born.

This contrast reached a climax in the Trojan War, where myth tells of Athena striking Ares down to stop his rampage in favor of the Trojans. Her blow was swift and precise, a triumph not just of power, but of purpose. In that moment, the gods themselves bore witness to the triumph of discipline over disorder, wisdom over wrath.

Yet even in defeat, Ares remained indispensable. He was the dark truth of conflict—the agony, rage, and ruin that shadowed every sword drawn. His clash with Athena did not diminish his role, but rather revealed the necessary turmoil at the heart of war. Together, their struggle shaped the Greek understanding of battle: a ceaseless tension between savage strength and sovereign skill.

Love in the Shadow of War

Though Ares stirred dread upon the battlefield and drew scorn from Olympus, he found a rare solace in the arms of Aphrodite, goddess of love and radiant desire. Their union, born of flame and longing, defied expectation—a tempestuous bond between beauty and bloodshed. In Aphrodite's embrace, the war god's fury gave way to passion, revealing a hidden tenderness beneath his armored form.

Their affair, veiled in secrecy, kindled even as Aphrodite remained wed to Hephaestus, the divine artisan. Their stolen moments were rich with fire and forbidden joy—a stark contrast to the clamor of war that so often trailed Ares's name. But love among the gods is seldom without consequence.

In one famed tale, Hephaestus, cunning and wounded, forged a snare of unbreakable chains. When the lovers lay entwined, his trap was sprung. He summoned the gods to bear witness, exposing their shame beneath the gaze of immortality. Laughter echoed through Olympus—not in cruelty alone, but in awe at the vulnerability of war and the unfaithfulness of love.

Yet even mocked, their bond endured. From their union sprang celestial children—Eros, the archer of desire, and Harmonia, bringer of balance—offspring that embodied the paradox of their love: beauty born of violence, harmony wrested from discord.

In Aphrodite, Ares was not tamed, but revealed. Their story deepened his myth, reminding mortals and immortals alike that love and war are not opposites, but twin forces entwined—each capable of wounding, each capable of wonder.

Mayhem and Wrath Unleashed

The Trojan War—epic in scope and steeped in sorrow—offered Ares a battlefield worthy of his tempestuous nature. As the god of war, he descended into the fray with armor gleaming and spear in hand, a divine embodiment of rage and ruin. Yet the very traits that made him formidable—impulse, pride, and unrestrained force— often sowed discord rather than victory.

Ares cast his lot with the Trojans, not out of loyalty or principle, but for bloodlust and the will of Aphrodite, who favored their cause. He waged war not as a tactician, but as a storm—fierce, blinding, and without direction. To the warriors beneath him, his presence stirred both awe and dread. Wherever he tread, shields splintered and the cries of the dying followed.

But brute strength alone could not shield him from defeat. In one famed clash, Ares met Diomedes, a mortal warrior strengthened by Athena's cunning. Guided by the goddess of strategy, Diomedes struck the war god with piercing force. Wounded and humiliated, Ares fled to Olympus, roaring in agony—proof that even divinity could falter when pitted against reason.

His constant clashes with Athena mirrored the war itself—chaos battling calculation, wrath against wisdom. While Athena shaped outcomes with foresight and purpose, Ares lunged with unchecked fury, often deepening the wounds he sought to avenge. His presence did not guide the war to resolution but rather magnified its ruin.

Yet Ares's role was far from hollow. He gave form to war's darkest truths—its capacity for suffering, its seduction of glory, and its cost in blood and soul. He did not ennoble battle; he revealed its savage core.

In the end, Ares emerges not as a god of triumph, but of truth. His myths—marked by rivalry, passion, and defeat—reflect the duality of conflict itself: strength tempered by vulnerability, courage corrupted by impulse. Though reviled and feared, he remains essential—a symbol of war's chaos and the untamed fire that burns within gods and mortals alike.

FORCE BEHIND THE FURY

Ares wielded the untamed fury of war itself, a force where chaos surged and bloodshed reigned. He did not guide with wisdom but inflamed the hearts of warriors, stirring frenzy, rage, and the will to conquer or perish. His presence on the battlefield summoned terror and valor in equal measure—a divine tempest that shattered order and glorified strife. As the patron of soldiers and slaughter,

Ares embodied the brutal majesty of combat, a god whose power both empowered the brave and devoured the reckless. He was the pulse of war unbound—glorious, ruinous, and eternally feared.

> *"Ares, who brings war to men and delight in the clash of arms, whose strength is as boundless as his rage."*
> — *Hesiod, Theogony*

Crimson God, Broken Fields

Ares, god of war and ruin, was the living pulse of battle's darkest fury—a force unchained and relentless. Unlike Athena, who wielded strategy and precision, Ares surged with raw brutality, the thunder of swords and the scream of the dying. He was the clash of iron, the blood in the dust, the storm that made mortals tremble and gods take heed.

In myth, he charged into battle cloaked in crimson armor, his spear glinting with promised death. His chariot, drawn by fire-breathing steeds, thundered across the field, scattering terror in his wake. Ares did not simply join battle—he was battle incarnate, exulting in carnage, reveling in the anarchy.

Yet his power was more than physical. He stirred the hearts of men to rage, igniting violence in their veins and driving them beyond fear or reason. Where Ares moved, discipline shattered and instinct ruled. He was the primal fire within warfare, a divine madness no shield could halt.

Still, Ares was no mindless brute. His presence, though feared, revealed a truth the Greeks could not deny: war is inevitable, and within its devastation lies the crucible of courage. Though destruction followed his path, so too did the forging of legends.

Ares stood as both scourge and spark—destroyer and awakener of valor. He reminded mortals that the battlefield was not just a place of ruin, but a forge where fate, fury, and fear gave rise to greatness. In him, the Greeks saw not only the terror of war—but its unyielding truth.

Bloodlust Unleashed

Among Ares's most fearsome gifts was his power to awaken bloodlust and unleash chaos, turning mortal hearts into engines of destruction. His influence was a double-edged blade—one that could forge heroes in fire or consume them in madness. This mystical frenzy mirrored Ares himself: wild, unrelenting, and forever untamed.

In the heart of battle, his presence moved like a shadowed wind. He whispered to warriors as they clashed, kindling a primal fury that drowned out fear. Under his spell, hesitation vanished, and reason gave way to the intoxication of violence. Muscles surged, weapons flew, and eyes burned with the thrill of conquest. Yet such power came at a cost—for many who tasted it lost not only their enemies, but themselves.

Ares's maelstrom did not end with the individual—it swept through entire legions. His spirit stirred insurrection and disarray, rupturing the order of war with eruptions of unpredictable force. Even the most disciplined ranks could unravel in his wake, as generals watched strategies collapse under the weight of fury. Ares did not merely fight battles; he transformed them into storms— savage, directionless, and soaked in ruin.

Yet in this bedlam, a deeper truth remained. His power, though terrifying, revealed the raw soul of conflict—the courage born of desperation, the rage sparked by loss, the glory clawed from ruin. Ares exposed the fire that burned beneath the armor, the brutal paradox at the heart of war: that greatness and devastation are often forged in the same flame.

His was a force to fear, but also to worship—for in every clash and cry, Ares reminded gods and mortals alike that chaos is not the enemy of war. It is its essence.

Champion of Valor

Though Ares was feared for his carnage and scorned by gods for his fury, to the warrior he was sacred. In him, soldiers saw not a destroyer alone, but a heavenly embodiment of courage—the unbreakable spirit needed to face steel, fire, and death. Ares was their champion, their protector, their god of grim resolve.

Before battle, warriors called his name in prayer and poured offerings upon his altars. They sought not peace, but power—strength for the arm, clarity for the strike, endurance for the storm ahead. In the stillness before combat, they reached for Ares, invoking his favor that their blades might not falter and their hearts might not fail. His temples stood as sacred ground for those bound by oath and shield, places where courage was sharpened like iron.

His patronage stretched beyond the lone fighter to the phalanx, the army, the city at war. In moments of crisis, whole communities turned to Ares, placing their fate in the hands of the war god. His likeness adorned shields and coins, his name etched into banners borne to the front—symbols of allegiance not to cruelty, but to the courage required to endure it.

Yet even in reverence, tension lingered. Ares's untamed nature clashed with the discipline of generals and the measured counsel of Athena. His glory came at a price, and not all who bore his favor survived to tell the tale. But his presence was undeniable—etched into the soul of every soldier who stepped onto blood-soaked earth.

Through his embodiment of violent conflict, his dominion over bloodlust and chaos, and his sacred bond with warriors, Ares stood as a god of profound duality. At once feared and revered, savage and noble, he revealed war's unflinching truth—a force that forged heroes as often as it destroyed them.

FACE OF THE BATTLEFIELD

Ares's influence in Greek culture reflected the brutal complexity of war—worshiped as a divine champion of valor, yet dreaded as the embodiment of unrestrained violence. His image, fierce and imposing in art, captured the raw energy he brought to every battlefield. The Greeks saw in him not just a god, but a mirror of conflict itself. His eternal contrast with Athena—instinct versus intellect, discord versus foresight—offered a deeper truth: that war, in all its terror and glory, demanded both passion and precision. Through Ares, they confronted the chaos that shaped both victory and ruin.

"Ares, bane of mortals, stained with blood of battle,
who delights in the clash of arms and the roar of war."
— Homer, The Iliad

Dread and Devotion

Among the ethereal figures of Greek myth, Ares stood as one of the most polarizing—both feared and honored, despised and desired. As the embodiment of war's chaos and fury, he stirred unease in the hearts of mortals and immortals alike. While Athena represented the wisdom of warfare, Ares raged as its unrestrained storm—raw violence without pretense, the clamor of blades and the blood-soaked earth. His presence reflected the uneasy reverence the Greeks held for war: a force to be feared, yet never ignored.

To the Hellenic mind, Ares was a necessary evil—summoned in desperation, respected with caution. Battle was inescapable, and his shadow loomed over every soldier who marched to war. Warriors cried out to him for strength, that they might stand unbroken before the enemy, even as they feared what his favor might unleash. Ares chose no side based on justice or cause—his loyalty lay with conflict itself, and his ferocity was as dangerous to friend as it was to foe.

Yet in places like Sparta, where martial valor was sacred, Ares found fervent devotion. There, he was not a destroyer but a paragon of strength—feral, fearless, and divine. His altars bore the trophies of conquest, his name invoked in rites of steel and blood. Spartan warriors saw in him their highest virtues: courage, aggression, and glory in death.

In this dual image—honored and hated, heavenly and monstrous—Ares revealed the soul of war. He was the god of man's darkest instincts and greatest trials, a mirror of the battlefield and the moral weight it carried. Through him, the Greeks confronted not only the cost of combat, but the conflict within themselves.

Form of Fury

Ares's image in Greek art surged with force and vitality, capturing the celestial ferocity that defined him. Sculptors and painters rendered him not only as a warrior, but as war made flesh—powerful, poised, and ever on the brink of violence. Clad in masterfully wrought armor and crowned with a helmet fit for a god, he radiated both physical perfection and untamed purpose. Each expression, each stance, pulsed with the wild energy that made Ares both feared and honored.

In marble, Ares often stood fully armed—helmeted, spear in hand, shield at his side—ready to spring into battle. The famed *Ares Ludovisi*, a Roman copy of a lost Greek original, portrays him in rare stillness: seated, contemplative, yet every line of his form brimming with restrained power. It is a portrait of the storm before it breaks, a god momentarily at rest but never at peace.

On painted pottery and frescoes, Ares erupted across the battlefield—his figure towering, his form fluid, his might unrelenting. Artists captured his relentless drive and martial grandeur, often placing him amid mortals or in the company of Aphrodite, blending themes of passion and bloodshed. In these scenes, he was more than a god—he was a symbol of momentum, of force ungoverned.

What made his representations so compelling was the tension between beauty and brutality. Ares's form was ideal, his face the image of youth and strength—yet his nature was storm-tossed and volatile. This contrast revealed the deeper truth of war: that behind its grandeur lies chaos, behind its glory, grief. Through brush and chisel, the Greeks gave shape to the paradox of Ares—a god who dazzled the eye even as he darkened the world.

Rage and Reason

Ares's place within the Greek pantheon was often cast in stark relief against that of his sister, Athena. Their mystic rivalry revealed the dual soul of war—one ruled by fury, the other by reason. Together, they embodied the eternal tension between raw aggression and calculated strategy, shaping the Greeks' understanding of conflict as both chaos and craft.

Ares charged into battle with a heart ablaze, led by instinct and consumed by the storm of violence. He sought not resolution, but release—war as a reckoning, a divine unleashing of primal force. For him, battle was the end in itself, a sacred frenzy where fear dissolved and fury reigned. Yet this passion, though mighty, rarely led to triumph—for Ares lacked the vision that turns conquest into legacy.

Athena, in contrast, moved with precision. She was the silent strategist, the weaver of victory before the first blade struck. Her warfare was purposeful, her mind as sharp as the spear she bore. Where Ares burned, Athena guided; where he destroyed, she rebuilt. Her victories emerged not from brute strength, but from foresight and balance, justice drawn through conflict.

Nowhere was this contrast more vivid than in the Trojan War. Ares, wild and unchecked, fought for the Trojans with a lust for blood. Athena, cool and cunning, shaped the fate of the Greeks with decisive interventions. Their encounters on the battlefield echoed a deeper struggle—the clash between impulse and intellect, destruction and discipline.

Even in their dealings with mortals, the divide held firm. Athena uplifted heroes, whispering wisdom to those who dared think before they struck. Ares kindled fear, igniting the rage that broke ranks and spilled blood. Yet both were vital. Through their rivalry, the Greeks understood that war, like life, was a balance of fury and thought—a fire that must burn, but never without purpose.

WRATH AND REVERENCE

Ares, god of war and wrath, remains one of the most enigmatic figures in the Greek pantheon—a deity as feared as he was essential. He embodied the untamed fury of battle, where order dissolved into chaos and steel answered only to instinct. Unlike Athena, who shaped war with reason and restraint, Ares thrived in the storm—his strength drawn from the clash of blades, the roar of rage, and the raw will to conquer. His myths paint him not as a hero, but as a force—reckless, relentless, and necessary in a world where conflict could never be avoided.

Within his stories, Ares reveals himself as more than a destroyer. In his affair with Aphrodite, we glimpse a god touched by longing and tenderness, vulnerable in love though fierce in war. On the fields of Troy, his reckless valor leads not to triumph but to retreat—yet even in failure, he remains a symbol of courage drawn from chaos. Warriors invoked his name not for wisdom, but for strength in the face of death, trusting the fire within him to light their own.

Ares's legacy endures not just in the myths of combat, but in the art, the symbols, and the eternal questions he stirred. He represents the double edge of war—glorious and ruinous, sacred and savage. His contrast with Athena completes the spectrum of conflict, revealing that both discipline and desire, foresight and fury, have their place in the theater of war. In every clash of will and steel, his legacy endures—not to glorify war, but to remind us of its price. As we now depart from the battlefield, we step into the realm of love and allure. In the next chapter, we turn to Aphrodite, goddess of beauty and desire, to explore her enchantments, her divine influence, and the timeless force that moves gods and mortals alike.

CHAPTER 10

APHRODITE

Goddess of Love and Beauty

Born from the shimmering foam of the sea, Aphrodite emerged as a divine enchantress—radiant, eternal, and perilous in her beauty. Her myths shimmer with both ecstasy and sorrow, revealing a goddess who did not merely embody love but commanded it with a force that could sway the heavens and unravel kings. From the fateful judgment of Paris, where her promise ignited a war, to her tender yet mournful bond with Adonis, each tale unveils her dual nature—nurturer of desire, harbinger of strife. Through her, passion became power, and beauty, a thread woven through the destinies of mortals and gods alike.

> *"Aphrodite, the golden,*
> *whose smile and beauty enchant gods and mortals alike,*
> *bringing love and desire wherever she treads."*
> *— Homeric Hymn to Aphrodite*

Seafoam and Sky

The origins of Aphrodite shimmer with divine mystery, as wondrous and beguiling as the goddess herself. Her birth was no mortal event, but a sacred upheaval—an alchemy of blood, sea, and sky. In the most famed of her legends, she rose not from womb or wombed earth, but from the sea itself, born of the brine that formed when the sky god Uranus was cast down by his son Cronus.

As Uranus fell, severed and defeated, his immortal essence spilled into the ocean depths. There, mingled with the churning tides, it birthed a celestial froth. From this mythic foam, Aphrodite emerged—fully formed, luminous, and resplendent. She drifted ashore upon the isle of Cyprus, where even the sand bloomed beneath her steps. The waters hushed in reverence. Flowers awakened. Birds lifted their songs. The very world turned toward her radiance.

Her birth was not merely an origin, but a revelation: the eternal power of beauty born through love, of creation summoned through yearning. She was not only lovely—she was the source of longing, the embodiment of attraction that binds all living things. Gods looked upon her and trembled. Mortals beheld her and were undone.

Thus began her mythic journey—not as a passive figure of charm, but as a force of cosmic magnitude. Aphrodite, sprung from sea and sky, bore with her the ancient gifts of union and seduction, of harmony and discord. From the foam, she carried the sacred flame of passion—capable of forging peace or inciting ruin with a single glance.

Apple and the Anemone

Among the many legends that unveil Aphrodite's power, two stand supreme in scope and sorrow: the judgment of Paris and the lament of Adonis. These myths unveil not just her influence, but her essence—a goddess who could ignite passion or plunge hearts into grief with equal ease. She is not simply a bringer of love, but a heavenly force whose desires ripple through time and fate.

The tale of Paris begins at a divine wedding, where Eris, goddess of discord, cast a golden apple into the feast—etched with a single promise: *To the fairest*. Hera, Athena, and Aphrodite claimed the prize, and the heavens fell silent as their rivalry flared. Unwilling to judge, Zeus turned the decision to Paris, prince of Troy, whose beauty and grace made him a fitting arbiter of such mythic rivalry.

The goddesses stood before him, each offering a gift: Hera promised dominion, Athena pledged victory, but Aphrodite whispered of Helen, mortal queen of unmatched beauty. Enchanted, Paris offered her the golden fruit, binding himself to destiny and awakening a storm of war. In winning the apple, Aphrodite claimed a mortal's heart—but at a cost that would consume nations. Her charm inspired love, but it could also unravel kingdoms. In that apple of discord lay the seed of war, for Paris's choice would one day burn Troy.

Yet another tale reveals a gentler sorrow. Adonis, a mortal born of astonishing beauty, stirred in Aphrodite not allure alone but devotion. She loved him deeply, fiercely, yet love could not shield him from fate. Struck down by a boar in the wild, Adonis died in her arms. Where her tears fell upon his blood, the anemone bloomed—a flower of grief, fleeting and delicate as love itself.

In some tellings, even Zeus was moved. He granted Adonis leave to return each year from the realm of the dead, a divine concession to love's endurance. Thus Adonis came to embody the cycles of nature—death and rebirth, sorrow and joy.

Together, these myths reveal the twin faces of Aphrodite: the enchantress who can set empires ablaze, and the mourner who weeps for the frailty of beauty. Through desire and loss, she reminds us that love is the most radiant of gifts—and the most devastating.

When Passion Ignited Destiny

Aphrodite's hand lay heavy upon the Trojan War, not through the sword but through the heart—her influence woven into its beginning, its cravings, and its tragedies. It was she who set the spark, offering Helen of Sparta as a divine bribe to Paris, the Trojan prince. From that vow, empires stirred, and blood stained the earth. A war of a thousand ships was not born of conquest, but of love promised and stolen.

Throughout the conflict, Aphrodite stood as guardian of the Trojans, shielding her favored mortals with ordained grace. Paris, her chosen, was snatched from death in a duel with Menelaus—spirited away by her unseen hand before the fatal blow could fall. To his enemies, it was cowardice; to Aphrodite, it was protection. Her loyalty to those she loved was unwavering, a force as fierce as the war itself.

Yet her presence was not only in deeds, but in hearts. Aphrodite stirred the emotions that drove men to glory or ruin. Love, lust, jealousy, longing—these were her weapons, as potent as any spear. In a war driven by pride and vengeance, it was her invisible influence that shaped the battlefield's fire.

She clashed often with Athena, her rival among the gods, whose intellect and strategy stood in opposition to Aphrodite's passion and instinct. Their immortal contest mirrored the war below—reason pitted against desire, order against chaos. The battlefield became a mirror of Olympus, where gods fought not only for mortals, but for their own truths.

Aphrodite's role in the Trojan War reveals the power of love not only to heal, but to destroy. She was the architect of longing and the bearer of grief, her duality manifest in every stolen glance and shattered oath. Her legacy in the war is one of beauty entangled with ruin, a reminder that love, when unleashed, can redraw the fates of nations.

Through every myth, Aphrodite stands as a goddess of unrelenting paradox—tender and perilous, adored and feared. From her foam-born birth to her shaping of mortal destiny, her influence lingers like perfume on the battlefield—haunting, divine, and unforgettable.

GIFTS OF THE HEART

Aphrodite's powers flowed through the hidden currents of love, beauty, and passion, shaping hearts and histories with hallowed ease. Her influence extended from Olympus to the mortal world, binding gods and men in passion's embrace. With her radiance, she stirred devotion and jealousy alike, weaving joy and sorrow into the tapestry of life. Aphrodite did not merely inspire affection—she commanded it, awakening forces that could unite kingdoms or tear them apart. Through her enchantments, she revealed the fragile balance between harmony and chaos, proving that the mightiest powers are often those that move unseen through the soul.

> *"She stirs sweet longing in the hearts of gods and men, and she subdues the reason and wise counsel of them all."*
> — *Hesiod, Theogony*

Dominion Over Desire

Aphrodite, radiant goddess of love and beauty, wielded a power that moved beyond the flesh and into the soul's hidden chambers. Her command over passion and attraction was unrivaled, granting her an influence that rivaled the mightiest Olympians. While others ruled through strength or strategy, Aphrodite's touch altered the course of fate with a glance, a sigh, a stirring of longing that no logic could withstand.

Her dominion reached far beyond romantic desire. Aphrodite governed all forms of allure—from the gentle trust of friendship to the thunderous pull of infatuation. She lived in the spark between strangers, the silent magnetism that tethered hearts, the longing that blurred reason and bound spirits. She could unite those fated to meet, mend love grown cold, and inspire bonds that endured beyond death's veil.

Much of her charm was woven into her enchanted girdle, a supernatural relic threaded with irresistible enchantments. When clasped around her form, it magnified her natural allure, bending the hearts of gods and mortals alike. Even Hera, queen of Olympus, once borrowed it to rekindle Zeus's affection—proof of Aphrodite's universal sway over the affections of even the most formidable.

Yet this sacred power was not without peril. As easily as she sowed affection, Aphrodite could fan the embers of jealousy, betrayal, and ruin. The love she awakened was not always gentle— it could smolder into obsession, fracture kingdoms, and turn joy into sorrow. Hers was a force both divine and dangerous, echoing the unpredictable nature of enchantment itself.

Through this formidable command over love and attraction, Aphrodite shaped not only the hearts of individuals but the fate of civilizations. She was a goddess who understood the sacred and the savage within longing, and whose legacy still lingers in every tale where hearts are stirred and destinies entwined.

Hearts Stirred, Fates Entwined

Aphrodite's influence coursed through every corner of the cosmos, touching gods and mortals with equal power. She was not merely a goddess of beauty—she was the force that stirred hearts, ignited desire, and unraveled the will of even the most resolute beings. Kings and craftsmen, warriors and weavers, Olympians and mortals alike found themselves entangled in the invisible threads she spun, threads woven not with might or wisdom, but with longing, allure, and irresistible charm.

Among the gods, her power was both revered and feared. Even Zeus, the ruler of the heavens, could not escape her reach. In one myth, she bent his affections toward mortal women, distracting him from Olympus and drawing his gaze toward the earthly realm. It was a quiet assertion of dominance—a reminder that love and desire, though intangible, could rival the thunderbolt in power.

Her ability to alter divine bonds extended far beyond courtship. Aphrodite shaped alliances, stoked jealousies, and deepened rivalries with a glance. Her role in the judgment of Paris—where she promised the love of Helen to the Trojan prince—did more than win a contest of beauty. It lit the spark of a war that would define an age, proving her capacity to steer destiny on a grand, destructive scale.

In the mortal world, her gifts carried equal weight. To those who pleased her, she offered irresistible charm, romantic triumph, and admiration that bordered on worship. But those who spurned her or slighted her name met her vengeance—a force subtle yet unrelenting. She elevated heroes, shattered lives, and shaped the course of legends.

One tale captures her mystery best: the story of Pygmalion, a sculptor who fell in love with his own creation. Moved by his devotion, Aphrodite breathed life into cold marble, transforming art into flesh, allure into reality. It was a miracle that revealed the full depth of her divinity—a goddess not of illusions, but of transformation.

Through every myth, Aphrodite proved that the heart, once stirred, could change the world. Her influence was not confined to fleeting passion, but echoed in the rise and fall of empires, the choices of gods, and the fate of souls.

Creation of Irresistible Beauty

At the heart of Aphrodite's divine power lay the ability to shape and embody irresistible beauty—a force that stirred the soul and awakened the senses. Her allure transcended mere appearance; it was a living expression of harmony, vitality, and sacred grace. Her radiance was not passive, but a power that compelled admiration, devotion, and longing from all who beheld her—gods and mortals alike.

Where Aphrodite walked, nature responded. Flowers unfurled in her presence, the air shimmered with unseen light, and joy stirred like a breeze through the hearts of those nearby. Her beauty was not still—it danced and breathed, inspiring artists to carve, paint, and compose in search of her elusive essence. Poets invoked her name, their verses woven with longing, drawn by the muse whose gaze could upend kingdoms.

Yet Aphrodite's gift extended beyond herself. With a touch, she could bestow beauty on others, cloaking mortals in charm that enchanted the world. In the myth of Paris, her promise of Helen's love was not only a reward of affection—it was the gift of heavenly beauty incarnate, a force potent enough to alter the fate of nations. Through such bestowals, Aphrodite shaped not only lives but legends.

But beauty, like fire, held danger. It could inflame envy, spark rivalry, and topple empires. The golden apple cast at the wedding of Peleus and Thetis—marked *"to the fairest"*—bore witness to this truth. The strife it unleashed led to war, proving that Aphrodite's gifts, while radiant, were never without consequence.

Her power revealed beauty's dual nature—glorious yet fleeting. Like blossoms kissed by dawn, it blooms only for a moment before fading. Aphrodite's presence was a reminder to cherish that brilliance while it lasts, for it echoes the eternal truth: all that is beautiful is also impermanent.

Through her control over love, her sway over gods and mortals, and her mastery of irresistible beauty, Aphrodite embodied a divine paradox—tender yet formidable, fleeting yet eternal. Her stories endure as testaments to the power of passion and the peril of desire, a goddess whose gifts shaped the very fabric of myth and memory.

LOVE IN LIFE AND LEGACY

Aphrodite's influence flowed through the heart of ancient Greek life, woven into the rituals, art, and poetry that honored her deific essence. Her worship was both grand and intimate—celebrated in majestic temples and sacred festivals, yet also in quiet offerings made with devotion and longing. As the goddess of love, beauty, and fertility, she was invoked in moments of passion and prayer alike. Her sacred symbols—the dove, the rose, the sea-born shell—made her presence visible, embodying the paradox of her power: gentle yet consuming, ephemeral yet everlasting. Through these expressions, Aphrodite left a radiant and eternal imprint on Greek culture.

> *"Aphrodite, who kindles sweet desire,*
> *and brings joy to gods and mortals alike,*
> *whose power none can resist."*
> — *Hesiod, Theogony*

Temples of Ardor and Devotion

Aphrodite's enchantment did not end with myth—it flourished in the embodied faithfulness of the ancient Greeks, who honored her through a radiant and widespread cult. As the divine embodiment of love, beauty, and fertility, she held a sacred station within Hellenic religion, her presence woven into daily rites and lifelong dreams. From bustling metropolises to tranquil village sanctuaries, her name echoed in prayers, her image adorned offerings, and her spirit was invoked in the rituals of longing and renewal.

Nowhere was her worship more resplendent than on the island of Cyprus, the sea-girt cradle of her birth. At Paphos, a grand sanctuary rose like a hymn in stone, its altars adorned with garlands and votive gifts from pilgrims who journeyed across the Aegean. Here, processions moved in rhythm to sacred hymns, and celebrants danced in reverence to the goddess who softened hearts and quickened life. The rituals of Paphos did not merely venerate her—they embodied her, channeling her sacred essence into the world.

Further west, atop the heights of the Acrocorinth, Aphrodite reigned as guardian of Corinth, presiding over love and the open sea. Her temple overlooked the harbor like a beacon, guiding sailors home and blessing merchants with fortune. Her birth from ocean foam made her the natural patroness of coastal realms, her protection sought in every venture that crossed the shifting tides.

Aphrodite's cult held a rare duality—sacred and sensual, celestial and carnal. In certain regions, her rites included sacred courtesans whose service was an act of reverence, expressing the generative power of love as a divine rite. Though alien to modern sensibilities, such practices were rooted in the belief that physical union, when blessed by the goddess, bridged the mortal and eternal.

Through her temples and ceremonies, Aphrodite was not merely worshipped—she was embodied. Her cult was a celebration of life's luminous pleasures and its most essential rhythms. In the rituals performed in her name, the ancients did not simply honor a goddess—they gave form to love itself, beauty sanctified, and desire raised to the level of the heavens.

Immortalized in Stone and Verse

Aphrodite's radiant beauty and divine allure stirred the hearts of artists and poets across the ancient world, making her one of the most enduring and exalted figures in Greek cultural expression. In marble and in meter, creators sought not merely to portray her form, but to evoke the sacred forces she represented—love, passion, and the eternal mystery of beauty.

In the realm of sculpture, she was rendered as the embodiment of feminine perfection, her figure balanced between sensuality and serenity. Most famed among these was the *Aphrodite of Knidos* by Praxiteles—a bold revelation in its time, depicting the goddess unveiled. This masterpiece, celebrated for its lifelike grace and goddess-born poise, set a new standard for the artistic portrayal of the human form and inspired generations of sculptors who followed. The statue's gaze, posture, and subtle gesture conveyed not only physical beauty but the radiant force that lingered within it.

Equally iconic was the *Venus de Milo*, a Hellenistic marvel whose quiet elegance continues to captivate. Draped in flowing garments that reveal as much as they conceal, she stands poised between movement and stillness, embodying the goddess's paradoxical nature—distant yet intimate, ethereal yet present.

In poetry, Aphrodite reigned as muse and mystery. The lyric poet Sappho of Lesbos, whose verses tremble with longing and devotion, invoked the goddess in hymns of desperate desire and divine compassion. Her surviving *Hymn to Aphrodite* paints the goddess not only as a celestial force but as a confidante of the heart, moved by mortal pleas and responsive to the ache of love unfulfilled.

Epic poets, too, gave Aphrodite form and influence. In the *Iliad* and *Odyssey*, Homer portrays her as a heavenly power whose beauty alters destinies and whose favor—or fury—can shape the course of empires. Her appearances within these epics reveal a goddess both revered and contested, one whose touch could lead to salvation or sorrow.

Through sculpture and poetry, Aphrodite was made eternal. Artists and poets did not merely depict her—they channeled her.

Their works shimmer with the same timeless allure she embodied, bearing witness to a goddess who stirred creation itself, and whose mythic legacy continues to enchant the world.

Emblems of Eternal Love

The sacred emblems of the dove and the rose echo the essence of Aphrodite's divinity, capturing her presence in both nature and ritual. Rooted in myth and revered in custom, these symbols became enduring reflections of her dual nature—gentle and fierce, fleeting and eternal.

The dove, often shown beside the goddess in sculpture and verse, symbolized peace, fidelity, and the quiet power of affection. Its soft gaze and graceful flight embodied the serenity Aphrodite bestowed upon those in love. As creatures of courtship and mating, doves mirrored her role as the eternal matchmaker, guiding hearts with invisible threads. During her festivals, flocks of doves were released into the sky, their ascension seen as a blessing from the goddess herself. Some were kept within temple sanctuaries, where their presence and song were offerings in motion—living vessels of Aphrodite's grace.

The rose, blooming with both beauty and sorrow, was no less sacred. According to myth, the first rose sprang from the mingled blood of Adonis and the tears of Aphrodite, a blossom born of love and lamentation. Its petals, delicate yet thorned, reflected the pleasure and peril of desire, the sweetness of love shadowed by the certainty of loss.

In rituals, roses adorned her altars and statues, scattered in devotion or woven into garlands to honor her divine charm. Their fragrance perfumed sacred spaces, a reminder of beauty's brief bloom and the passions it awakens. In art, Aphrodite is often depicted bearing a rose, her hand cradling both creation and fragility, life and longing.

Together, the dove and the rose spoke a silent language, expressing what words could not—the serenity and storm of love, the purity of peace, and the ache of beauty's impermanence. Through them, Aphrodite's essence lingered in every petal and every wingbeat, her legacy carried not only in myth but in the living world.

GODDESS WHO SHAPED DESIRE

Aphrodite, goddess of love and radiant beauty, remains one of the most mesmerizing figures in Greek mythology. Her stories unveil a sacred force whose influence reached far beyond mere attraction, shaping destinies and altering the course of gods and mortals. From her birth upon the foam of the sea to her role in igniting the Trojan War, Aphrodite's power shimmered as both blessing and burden—capable of uniting hearts and unraveling empires.

Her presence echoed through every corner of ancient Greek life, celebrated in marble and verse, temple and ritual. The dove and the rose—symbols sacred to her name—captured the essence of her nature: tender yet consuming, ephemeral yet eternal. Artists and poets labored to preserve her divine allure, and in doing so, etched her legacy into the soul of Western imagination.

Yet Aphrodite was not a goddess of simplicity. Love, in her grasp, was no gentle muse. It could heal and uplift, but also deceive, divide, and destroy. Her myths remind us that desire is a double-edged flame—capable of forging devotion or lighting the path to ruin.

And now, as we turn from the goddess of longing and light, we descend into the forge of Mount Olympus to meet Hephaestus—the celestial artisan whose mastery of fire and metal shaped the marvels of the gods. Where Aphrodite charmed with beauty, Hephaestus labored in flame, crafting wonders that bound Olympus together with hammer and anvil.

CHAPTER 11

HEPHAESTUS

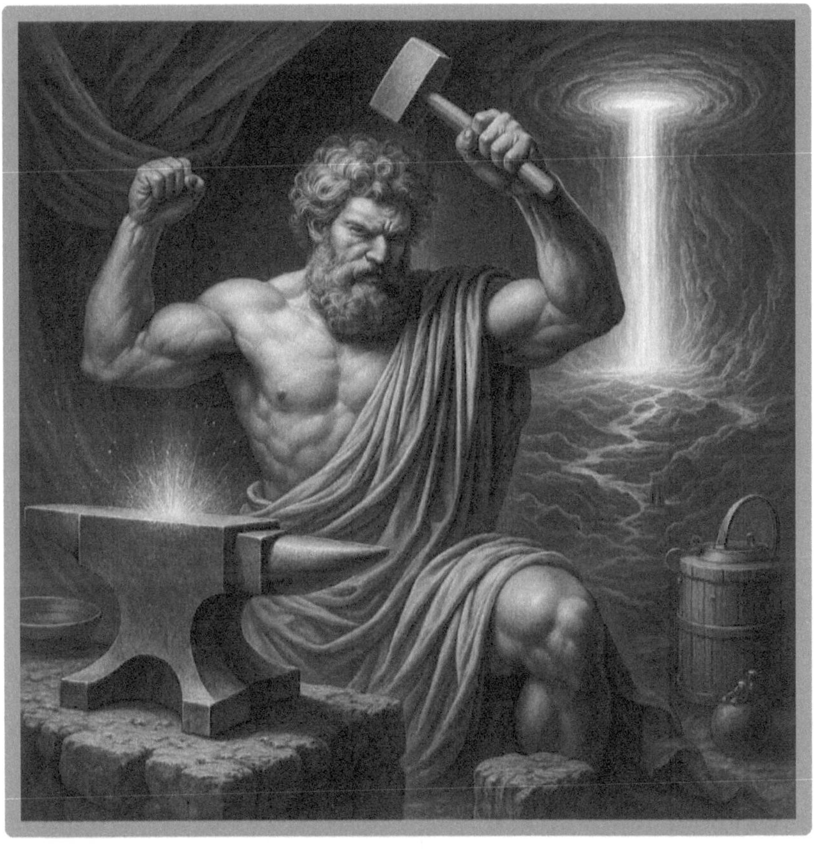

God of Forge and Fire

Hephaestus's myth weaves together themes of Godly rejection, endurance, and creative might, revealing a deity who rose from ruin to carve his place among the immortals. Cast from Olympus for his imperfection, he fell from the heavens not in defeat but into destiny. From this brutal descent, he rose not as a warrior but as a master artisan, his forge glowing with redemption. His union with Aphrodite, radiant yet fraught, echoed the contrast between outer beauty and inner worth. Through fire and craft, he shaped thrones, shields, and chains—artifacts of wonder born not from favor but from resolve. In Hephaestus, the ancients saw not weakness, but a sacred truth: that greatness fashioned in adversity bears the mark of the exalted.

> *"Hephaestus, famed for skill,*
> *whose forge blazes beneath the earth,*
> *crafting wonders of metal and fire*
> *for gods and heroes alike."*
> *— Homer, The Iliad*

From the Heavens to the Abyss

Hephaestus, celestial master of flame and forge, came into the world with a fate as hammered and searing as the anvils he would one day command. Born of Hera alone—queen of Olympus, sovereign of storming wrath—his conception was wrought not in love, but in defiance. Scorned by Zeus's betrayals, Hera summoned life without him, birthing a son shaped by her will. Yet when her gaze fell upon the infant god, she recoiled. He bore not the radiant symmetry of the immortals, but a crooked form, marked by lameness—a flaw she could not bear to claim.

In a surge of immortal shame and fury, Hera seized the newborn and hurled him from the heights of Olympus. He plummeted from the heavens, a god cast down before he could rise. The sea caught him in its depths, and there, among the veiled currents, two sea goddesses—Thetis and Eurynome—lifted him from the abyss. In their secret grotto beneath the waves, far from deific judgment, Hephaestus found refuge. Within that ocean-shadowed sanctuary, he began to shape the world anew—not with vengeance, but with fire and craft. Coral, metal, and stone became his language. Solitude became his crucible.

Though rejected by his sacred bloodline, Hephaestus did not shatter. He was tempered like the blades he would one day create. From the furnace of disgrace, he rose not in vengeance, but in mastery. The forge became his throne, his hammer his scepter. And in time, the Olympians would behold the splendor of his works— armor gleaming with enchantments, royal seats etched with hidden power—and they would call him back. Thus, the god once cast away returned crowned in skill, proving that from exile, greatness may yet be brought to form.

Bond of Beauty and Flame

Hephaestus's return to Olympus did not herald peace, but another trial—one not of flame or furnace, but of the heart. By decree of Zeus, the god of fire was wed to Aphrodite, the goddess of love and beauty, in a union as unlikely as it was fateful. Where Hephaestus toiled in solitude and soot, she shimmered with allure and desire, a celestial flame who turned the eyes of gods and mortals alike. Their marriage was not born of passion, but of

Olympus's will—a pairing of labor and longing, craftsmanship and charm.

To Hephaestus, it was a heavenly hope fulfilled—a chance to bind his lonely soul to the most radiant of goddesses. But for Aphrodite, the forge offered no warmth. Her heart kindled not for the smith, but for Ares, the war-god whose fury mirrored her own burning spirit. Thus, from the start, their bond was strained— beauty and brilliance misaligned, and desire adrift.

When whispers reached Hephaestus of Aphrodite's secret entanglement with Ares, he turned not to thunder or rage, but to mastery. In the silence of his workshop, he wrought a snare of gold—an invisible net of mystic intricacy, unbreakable and unseen. He draped it across Aphrodite's bedchamber, and when the illicit lovers met, they were caught fast in its gleaming web. With deliberate grace, Hephaestus summoned the gods, unveiling the entangled pair to the heavens—not with vengeance, but with cold, unflinching revelation.

The act immortalized his cunning, yet laid bare his isolation. His triumph in craftsmanship could not mend the wounds of love denied. Though honored among gods for his skill, Hephaestus remained an outsider at heart—his genius forged in fire, his longing sealed in silence. In his story, the myths speak not only of betrayal, but of a soul seeking warmth in a world that revered his hands, yet overlooked his heart.

Creations of an Exalted Artisan

Though Hephaestus's heart bore the scars of betrayal and exile, his hands shaped wonders that no god or mortal could rival. In the roaring depths beneath the earth—where fire surged like divine breath and anvils rang like thunder—he brought to form the sacred lifeblood of Olympus. His foundry, hidden beneath a volcano's crown, blazed as the womb of creation, a realm where molten metal obeyed his will and vision became reality.

Hephaestus was the architect of gods. Halls gleamed with his designs, thrones bore his intricate mark, and weapons of legend passed through the heat of his furnace. None, perhaps, more famous than the armor of Achilles—fashioned for the hero of Troy at the behest of Thetis. The shield alone shimmered with cosmic artistry: stars and cities, fields and feasts, war and peace, all etched in hallowed precision. It was not merely protection, but prophecy—warrior and world, encircled in bronze.

At Zeus's command, Hephaestus shaped Pandora—the first mortal woman—from clay touched by immortal breath. She was wondrous to behold, her form carved with grace and mystery, yet within her vessel she bore the woes of humankind. Though the creation was born of another's will, it was Hephaestus who gave it form—his artistry entwined with mortal destiny.

To Hera, his mother and betrayer, he gifted a golden throne wrought with cunning. Upon it, she was elevated—and ensnared. Bound by mechanisms only he understood, she sat powerless, until pleas and promises brought Hephaestus back into Olympus's embrace. This device, both offering and revenge, marked a moment of reckoning—his pain transmuted into design.

While the ancient Cyclopes once ruled the forge, it was Hephaestus who gave Godly craftsmanship its soul. He fashioned the Aegis for Zeus, a mantle of terror crowned with Medusa's petrifying gaze. For Artemis and Apollo, he wrought bows of celestial might, fated to fell mortals and monsters alike. And within his furnace, he gave life to golden automatons—beings of metal and mind, silent servants of a god who labored alone.

In every creation, Hephaestus inscribed a portion of his story—his exile, his genius, his longing. From weapons of war to marvels of peace, he shaped the tools of gods and the fate of myths. Through fire, solitude, and invention, he transformed the forgotten into the indispensable. His legacy endures as proof that even in suffering, brilliance may be born—and that the divine lies not only in beauty, but in the will to create.

ANVIL OF PROGRESS

Hephaestus wielded the sacred fire with transcendent purpose, fusing destruction and creation into a single, eternal force. From the heart of volcanoes, he summoned flame to create weapons, thrones, and wonders for gods and heroes alike. His mastery of metalwork shaped the armor of Achilles, the Aegis of Zeus, and automatons with minds of their own. Yet his greatest power lay not in fire or steel, but in resilience—the hallowed spark to transform rejection into genius. Through every artifact he made, Hephaestus proved that creation is its own kind of immortality.

> "Hephaestus, the renowned craftsman,
> who with skillful hands fashions wondrous works,
> whose forge brings forth the light of invention."
> — Hesiod, Theogony

Dominion of Fire and Metal

Hephaestus, god of fire and deific craftsmanship, possessed a mastery over flame and metal that stood unrivaled among mortals or gods. His command of the smithy furnace was not merely skill, but the very expression of his immortal essence. Fire—the primal force of transformation and creation—obeyed him as if by birthright. In his hands, it did not consume, but revealed; it did not destroy, but transfigured. Through spark and flame, Hephaestus shaped the will of Olympus into form, becoming the supreme artisan of the celestial realm.

His workshop, often envisioned as a blazing cavern beneath the earth or hidden within the heart of a volcano, was a place where sacred flame met raw substance. It was here, surrounded by roaring heat and ringing anvils, that his genius unfolded. Bronze, gold, silver, and adamant were molded as easily as clay, their rigid nature softened by the mythic rhythm of his hammer. Every blow echoed with purpose, every spark carried the breath of invention. His tools did not merely aid him—they were conduits of Godly will, instruments through which creation passed into reality.

Metallurgy, in the hands of Hephaestus, became more than craft; it became sorcery. He knew the secrets of alloys, the temper of steel, the voice of every metal drawn from the bones of Gaia. The elements responded to him, as if recognizing their master. Objects born from his forge bore not only beauty and power, but soul—a legacy of the god who made them.

This sacred dominion over fire and metal reflected the essence of Hephaestus himself: scarred yet indomitable, humbled yet supreme. Flame could sear or sanctify, and like the god it obeyed, it carried the mystery of opposing forces. From heat and hardship,

Hephaestus shaped not only weapons and wonders—but the very myth of resilience.

Armorer of Olympus, Shaper of Power

Among the many marvels of Hephaestus's heavenly gift, none were more wondrous than his ability to hammer out the sacred weapons and tools of the gods. These were not mere instruments of war or labor—they were living symbols of dominion and myth, each one breathed into being with the precision of a master and the vision of a god. Through his creations, Hephaestus altered the balance of Olympus, equipping immortals and heroes alike with relics that bent the course of fate.

For Zeus, the king of gods, he crafted the Aegis—a shield wrought in awe and terror. Embellished with the petrifying face of Medusa, it inspired dread in the hearts of enemies and stood as a bulwark against chaos. In its design, Hephaestus united raw might with elegant form, creating not just protection but proclamation: the emblem of exalted supremacy.

To Artemis, huntress of the moonlit wilds, he gifted a silver bow and arrows—sleek, silent, and deadly. For Apollo, her twin, he fashioned a golden bow, whose string could unleash both wrath and rapture, channeling the sun's blaze or the muse's song. In each weapon, he captured the essence of its bearer—blending purpose, poetry, and mythic fire.

Beyond arms, Hephaestus sculpted the very tools of cosmic function. The chariot of Helios, which drew the sun across the heavens, gleamed with his craftsmanship. Hera's throne, intricate and radiant, bore his secret mechanisms. Each object, no matter its purpose, bore the sacred mark of Olympus's smith.

Even mortals knew his legacy. The armor of Achilles, fashioned in the sacred furnace at Thetis's request, bore the stories of the cosmos—its shield a universe in relief. Through his hearth, Hephaestus became not only a craftsman, but a creator of destiny. In every artifact, his divine artistry whispered the might of gods and the enduring power of creation.

Beneath the Mountain

Hephaestus's command over fire extended far beyond the confines of his celestial furnace. His dominion reached into the very bones of the earth—into the molten veins of volcanoes, where creation and destruction merged in sacred rage. These blazing mountains were not seen by the ancients as mere geological wonders, but as living altars of the forge-god himself. Their thunderous eruptions and rivers of molten flame were interpreted as signs of his divine labor, echoing through the world with heat, light, and awe.

Nowhere was this mythic bond more vividly realized than in the tale of Mount Etna. Towering above the Sicilian landscape, this volcano was believed to house one of Hephaestus's great subterranean workshops. There, deep within the mountain's heart, he was said to labor tirelessly, aided by the Cyclopes—his one-eyed brethren of fire and stone. When lava burst forth and ash darkened the sky, it was not destruction alone; it was the sound of hammer upon anvil, the hiss of metal meeting flame, and the sacred birth of divine creations. Each eruption was a revelation—molten testimony to the god's ongoing work.

To command a volcano was to wield both terror and transformation. In this elemental force, Hephaestus found his perfect symbol. Fire, uncontrolled, could devour forests and cities.

But in the hands of the smith-god, it became the crucible of beauty, invention, and radiant will. His mastery over volcanoes was not an act of domination, but one of sacred cooperation—an ancient harmony between creator and chaos.

Volcanoes themselves mirrored Hephaestus's spirit. Born from the deep, marked by pressure, they rose scarred but mighty—just as he had. Their eruptions, though fierce, also brought rebirth: fertile soils, new lands, reshaped worlds. They were reminders that from destruction could spring life, and from agony, brilliance.

Through his bond with these fiery mountains, Hephaestus stood not only as Olympus's master craftsman, but as a symbol of nature's raw and relentless creativity. His forge did not end at the anvil; it encompassed the world itself. The god beneath the mountain shaped more than artifacts—he shaped the mythic rhythm of the earth, where every flame told a story, and every eruption echoed with the sound of heavenly creation.

FORGE OF CIVILIZATION

Hephaestus's legacy was etched into the very soul of ancient Greece, his sacred fire reflected in the clang of anvils and the gleam of bronze. Temples rose in his honor, and workshops flourished under his patronage, where mortal artisans sought to channel his beloved craft. In the epics of Homer, he stood as a figure of resilience and ingenuity—flawed, yet exalted—whose mastery bridged the realms of god and man. He was the deific patron of blacksmiths, the unseen hand behind both sacred relics and mythic destinies. Through his transformative art, Hephaestus symbolized the power of creation not only to shape metal, but to mold fate itself—proving that even from fire and fracture, beauty and power could be born.

> *"Hephaestus, who with cunning skill creates works of wonder, whose forge never rests, and whose hands shape metal into marvels."*
> — Homer, The Iliad

Sanctuaries of Fire and Craft

Hephaestus, the immortal artisan, was venerated across the Greek world as the divine spark behind creation itself—the god who transfigured fire and metal into marvels of beauty and power. Temples raised in his honor were not only sanctuaries of worship, but tributes to the noble art of craftsmanship. These hallowed spaces stood as enduring symbols of the bond between celestial inspiration and human innovation, celebrating the god who bestowed form and function upon the cosmos.

Foremost among these was the Temple of Hephaestus in Athens, rising above the Agora like a monument to sacred industry. Built in the 5th century BCE and adorned with sculpted friezes depicting heroic myths and immortal labors, it enshrined the legacy of a god whose hands shaped the destiny of gods and men. Its preservation through the centuries is a testament to the reverence Athens held for the lord of the forge—a city that found in Hephaestus the divine reflection of its own cultural brilliance.

More than a site of ritual, the temple embodied the values Hephaestus represented: perseverance, precision, and the transformative power of creation. In a city renowned for its art and architecture, his influence was not distant—it pulsed through every chisel stroke and molten pour. The temple reminded Athenians that every masterpiece bore the echo of mythic craftsmanship.

Beyond Athens, shrines and workshops devoted to Hephaestus could be found throughout Greece, particularly on the island of Lemnos, where the god was said to have fallen from Olympus. There, amid volcanic terrain and ancient fire, his cult flourished. The people of Lemnos honored Hephaestus not as an aloof Olympian, but as a radiant presence rooted in their land—a symbol of resilience formed in flame.

These temples and sacred workshops were not static monuments; they were living intersections of faith, labor, and inspiration. In venerating Hephaestus, the Greeks celebrated the transcendent power of the forge and the creative spirit within themselves. Through him, they honored the eternal truth that from raw matter—and through toil—wonders are born.

Deific Smith in Epic Verse

Within the sweeping verses of Homer's epics, Hephaestus stands not only as the divine smith of Olympus but as a figure of quiet power and profound influence—his presence shaping the course of myth and the fate of mortals. In both the *Iliad* and the *Odyssey*, he emerges as a deity of complexity: brilliant, wounded, and indispensable.

In the *Iliad*, Hephaestus's role burns brightest in the wake of Achilles's grief. When Thetis, mother of the fallen hero, seeks aid for her son, she turns to Hephaestus—not for words of comfort, but for a gift only he can give: armor born of flame and genius. What follows is a divine act of creation. In the solitude of his workshop, Hephaestus crafts weapons of legend, but the shield of Achilles surpasses them all. More than defense, it is vision—a gleaming cosmos wrought in bronze. Cities in peace and war, plowed fields and dancing children, courts and harvests—all etched in immortal relief. Through this artifact, Hephaestus becomes a storyteller, capturing the duality of existence—joy and sorrow, struggle and serenity—upon the hero's arm.

His work does more than arm Achilles; it reminds the reader that even in war, the craft of the god shapes meaning, not just survival. The shield becomes a mirror of mortal life, each scene struck in metal as delicately as a poem—its beauty born from the hands of one cast aside, yet revered for his mastery.

In the *Odyssey*, Hephaestus reappears in song, not in solemnity but in satire. A bard recounts the tale of his ill-fated marriage to Aphrodite and her betrayal with Ares. Yet even here, the god of the forge does not rage—he plots. With cunning and precision, he hammers out an invisible net, ensnaring the lovers in an act of heavenly justice. The laughter of the gods may echo in jest, but beneath it lies a deeper truth: Hephaestus, though mocked and maligned, commands respect through wit and invention.

Through these epic moments, Hephaestus proves that his strength lies not in stature but in spirit. His creations alter destiny, and his presence bridges beauty and burden. In Homer's verse, he is more than a craftsman—he is the enduring fire beneath the myth.

Passed to Mortal Hands

Hephaestus, god of fire and the forge, left an indelible mark on the ancient world—not only in myth, but in the lives and labors of those who shaped metal with fire. To the blacksmiths of Greece, he was more than a distant deity; he was patron, exemplar, and kindred spirit. His mythic journey from rejection to reverence mirrored the toil of mortal artisans whose skill created the very tools of civilization.

In the blazing heat of their furnaces, blacksmiths saw reflections of the god. Like Hephaestus striking bronze beneath Mount Etna, they labored with hammer and flame to transform raw ore into weapons, armor, and artistry. His story inspired perseverance—proof that brilliance could rise from adversity, and that even scarred hands could craft objects worthy of gods. Their work was not mundane labor; it was a sacred echo of the god's own craft, infused with pride, purpose, and reverence.

Across the Greek world, Hephaestus was honored in festivals and rites devoted to fire and creation. Processions celebrated the mythic smith, offerings were made in thanks, and competitions of craftsmanship allowed artisans to display their mastery. In honoring Hephaestus, blacksmiths sought more than favor—they affirmed their connection to the sacred act of creation.

His influence extended beyond the flame-lit walls of the workshop. In myth, the objects Hephaestus breathed into being—shields, thrones, traps, and automatons—were more than functional; they were symbols, embodiments of power, precision, and beauty. This union of utility and elegance became a defining trait of Greek art and architecture, where even the most practical object was tempered with exalted intention.

The very idea of the forge—a place of transformation, where chaos becomes form—came to represent the creative spirit of humankind. To craft was to imitate the gods; to mold, to temper, to shape was to walk in Hephaestus's path. His legacy lived in every ringing hammerstroke and glowing blade, in every artisan who found dignity in the flame.

In this way, Hephaestus's myth passed from Olympus into the hands of mortals, shaping not only metal but culture itself. Through fire and craft, he became an eternal emblem of creation—divine, enduring, and forged in resilience.

LAST EMBER OF THE FORGE

Hephaestus, the mythic smith of Olympus, was a god whose legacy was not born of splendor, but brought to form in flame and endurance. His myths unveil a deity shaped by exile and struggle, yet exalted through creation—a master artisan whose brilliance rose from the ashes of rejection. From his fall from Olympus to the silent fire of his furnace, from the pain of betrayal to the splendor of immortal craft, Hephaestus embodied both the burden of imperfection and the triumph of unyielding skill.

The forge was his sanctum, the anvil his altar. There, in the hidden places beneath the earth, he transformed raw elements into hallowed marvels—Pandora's form, Achilles' armor, the thrones of Olympus, and the very shield that held the cosmos in bronze. His hands shaped more than tools; they molded fate. His story is not one of might, but of mastery—of how the overlooked god became the architect of legend, the soul of sacred invention.

Hephaestus reminds us that greatness is not always adorned in glory. Sometimes, it is born in fire—quiet, relentless, and essential.

From adversity, he fashioned beauty. From silence, he hammered meaning. He remains a symbol of resilience, creation, and the power of craft to elevate the soul.

And now, we leave the glowing embers of the forge and follow the wind-swept path of Hermes—the fleet-footed herald of Olympus. Where Hephaestus worked in fire and form, Hermes weaves through words, deception, and celestial speed. In the next chapter, we uncover the myths and mysteries of this elusive trickster, guide of souls and messenger of gods, whose cleverness shaped the heavens and the earth alike.

CHAPTER 12

HERMES

Messenger of the Gods

The myths of Hermes reveal a god of ethereal cunning, fluid boundaries, and radiant charm. From his daring theft of Apollo's cattle to the invention of the lyre, Hermes turned transgression into art, mischief into meaning. As shepherd of souls to the underworld, he moved with grace between realms, a bridge between life and death, gods and mortals. Trickster and messenger, inventor and mediator, Hermes embodied the power of transition—ever shifting, ever wise. His stories reflect a primordial surge unbound by walls or rules, where wit triumphs, harmony is restored, and the journey itself becomes sacred.

> *"Hermes, the swift-footed messenger of the gods, whose cunning and speed carry the will of Zeus to the ends of the earth."*
> — *Homer, The Iliad*

Theft That Sang to the Gods

Hermes entered the world not with cries, but with crafty grace—the infant god born of wit, speed, and Godly mischief. His mother, Maia, a shy and reclusive daughter of Atlas, gave birth to him in a shadowed cave nestled in the Arcadian hills. She sought solitude, hoping to shield her child from the gaze of Olympus. But even in that hidden cradle, greatness stirred. Born of Zeus and shaped by fate, Hermes was no ordinary newborn. He opened his eyes with purpose and took his first breath as though already plotting.

Within hours of his birth, he slipped free from his swaddling and wandered beyond the cave's mouth. The world greeted him with opportunity. There, he beheld a herd of sacred cattle—belonging to none other than Apollo, his radiant half-brother. A gleam of devilry danced in his gaze. What followed was not mere theft, but the birth of legend. Hermes devised a plan both brazen and brilliant, a trick that would bewilder gods and bards alike.

He led the cattle backward, reversing their tracks, and crafted sandals of bark and leaves to disguise his own. These deceptions, clever and seamless, rendered pursuit nearly impossible. Once the herd was hidden within a remote cave, Hermes returned to Arcadia, curled into his cradle, and cloaked himself once more in infantile stillness.

But Apollo's vision pierced shadows and riddles. Discovering the loss, he followed subtle signs to Maia's cave. There, he found a child—barely a day old—who met his accusations with charm, laughter, and innocent denial. Brought before Zeus, Hermes spun a tale so artful and amusing that even the king of gods could not help but smile. Yet justice demanded restitution.

To make peace, Hermes offered a gift—the lyre, his first invention, shaped from a tortoise shell and strung with sinews. Its music enchanted Apollo, and harmony replaced rage. The trickster and the sun-god were reconciled, and in that moment, a bond was conceived not through power, but through art.

In this tale of birth and boldness, Hermes claimed his place among the Olympians—not through might, but through mind. He was the god of boundaries, invention, and persuasion—ever-shifting, ever-clever, and destined to walk the roads between worlds.

Usher of Souls, Walker Between Worlds

Beyond the laughter of trickery and the swiftness of his stride, Hermes held a role sacred and solemn—psychopomp, the divine guide of souls. Among the Olympians, only he could walk freely between the realms of gods and men, the living and the dead. This power, both mysterious and merciful, marked him as a mediator of worlds and a guardian of thresholds.

As the messenger of Olympus, Hermes crossed divine boundaries with ease, his winged sandals carrying him from the heights of Mount Olympus to the depths of mortal despair. But when a soul released its final breath, it was Hermes who stood beside it—not with fear, but with grace. He led the newly departed along shadowed paths toward the underworld, past the whispering rivers and gates of no return, ensuring each spirit reached the domain of Hades in peace.

Where Hades ruled in silence and judgment, Hermes moved with quiet compassion. His presence at the hour of death offered comfort—not condemnation. The caduceus he bore, twin serpents entwined in harmony, symbolized his role: protector, healer, and bearer of transition. To the dying, he brought not dread, but a final companion—a divine escort into the unknown.

His role as psychopomp revealed the deeper soul of Hermes, one attuned to the impermanence of all things. He was the patron of crossroads, travelers, and beginnings—but also of farewells. Just as he delivered messages across Olympus, so too did he carry souls across the veil. He understood that life and death were not enemies, but partners in a spiritual cycle—and he alone could move between them without fear.

This sanctified duty elevated Hermes beyond mischief and speed. In the hush between heartbeats and the silence beyond breath, he became a conductor of mercy—a light for those journeying into shadow. In this role, Hermes reminded gods and mortals alike that even in death, there is motion, there is passage, and there is a hand to lead the way.

Music Born from Mischief

On the very day Hermes stole Apollo's sacred cattle, another marvel was born—one not of trickery, but of music. In a moment of inspired wonder, Hermes created the lyre, a gift of sound and soul, and a symbol of transformation through exalted artistry. What began as playful curiosity would echo through Olympus and the world of mortals, shaping a legacy not with theft, but with harmony.

While wandering through the wilds of Arcadia, Hermes came upon a tortoise and perceived more than a creature—he saw a vessel of melody. With mythic ingenuity, he hollowed the shell and stretched across it strings made from sheep gut. As his fingers brushed the cords, the instrument sprang to life, its tones weaving joy and sorrow into one celestial voice. The music that rose from it was not merely beautiful—it was alive, stirring the air with rhythms that spoke to gods and mortals alike.

The lyre was more than invention—it was transformation. Hermes had turned the ordinary into the radiant, proving his gift for creation as powerful as his gift for cunning. With this act, he revealed that the same mind that devised tricks could also shape wonders, and that beauty often blooms from unexpected places.

Seeking to mend the rift with Apollo, Hermes offered the lyre as a token of reconciliation. The sun-god, master of song and prophecy, was moved by the music's purity. He accepted the gift, his anger cooled by melody, and in return bestowed upon Hermes the golden caduceus—his emblem of peace, wisdom, and balance. From this exchange rose not rivalry, but respect, a divine accord sealed by art.

Beyond myth, the lyre would endure as a symbol of Greek culture—a sacred bridge between human emotion and divine resonance. It became the voice of poets, the soul of ceremonies, the thread that bound community and spirit. Through the lyre, Hermes left a mark not in stone, but in song—a legacy not of dominion, but of inspiration.

GODLY MESSENGER

The powers of Hermes shimmered with motion, wit, and transformation—each a facet of his divine mastery over change. With unmatched speed and a voice that bridged heaven and earth, he served as the swift messenger of the gods. Yet he was also the guardian of travelers, merchants, and all who moved between realms, offering protection in moments of passage. As trickster and shapeshifter, he wielded cleverness like a blade—unmasking truth through illusion and turning chaos into opportunity. In every role, Hermes revealed the sacred art of transition, proving that to move swiftly is also to see deeply, and to adapt is to endure.

> *"Hermes, the bringer of good luck,*
> *the swift messenger of the gods,*
> *whose wand brings sleep and whose*
> *voice guides the souls of the dead."*
> — *Homeric Hymn to Hermes*

Swift Voice of Olympus

Among the many charms of Hermes, none shone brighter than his speed—a transcendent swiftness that made him the eternal thread between gods and mortals. His winged sandals, the Talaria, forged by Hephaestus, were not mere tokens of flight, but sacred tools of movement and momentum. With them, Hermes traversed the sky, the earth, and the shadowed lands below, crossing thresholds no other could pass. His speed was not measured in distance, but in purpose—the swift bearer of fate and voice of the immortals.

As messenger of the gods, Hermes was indispensable. With words wrapped in wind, he delivered Zeus's decrees, carried omens to heroes, and stirred mortal hearts with guidance or warning. He moved unseen in moments of crisis, whispering resolution into the storm. His swiftness bridged realms—Olympus, Earth, and Hades—binding them in sacred motion. Yet his greatest strength was not in how fast he traveled, but in what he carried: words that shaped the cosmos, messages that mended the world.

In the tale of Persephone, when Demeter grieved and the earth withered under sorrow, it was Hermes whom Zeus entrusted. He descended into Hades not with threat, but with reason. Through his presence and persuasion, Persephone was granted return—a cycle of death and rebirth, winter and spring, sorrow and renewal. Thus, Hermes's flight became more than movement; it was diplomacy made heavenly.

Beyond Olympus's errands, Hermes embodied the flow of information, thought, and expression. He was the patron of eloquence, the spirit of persuasion, the breath behind every clear word and thoughtful reply. His voice calmed anger, brokered peace, and illuminated paths unseen. Where there was confusion, he brought clarity. Where there was distance, he built bridges.

To speak with Hermes's tongue was to hold power—not of conquest, but of connection. In every myth where he runs, flies, or speaks, Hermes reminds us that swiftness alone is nothing without understanding, and that true speed is measured not in haste, but in harmony.

Protector of Roads, Friend of Trade

The celestial swiftness of Hermes did not serve only the gods—it guided mortals across uncertain paths and open seas. As the patron of travelers and merchants, Hermes became a beacon of movement, protection, and exchange. In a world where every journey bore risk—where roads wound through wild lands and unseen dangers lurked in shadow—his presence offered a sacred shield. He was the god invoked at the start of every voyage, the silent companion at every crossroads, and the unseen hand that cleared the path ahead.

Along the dusty highways of Greece, travelers paused at roadside shrines called herms—stone pillars bearing Hermes's likeness and sigils. These sacred markers served both spirit and sense: talismans to ward off misfortune and guideposts through unfamiliar lands. To offer a stone, coin, or prayer at a herm was to summon the favor of the guiding-god, seeking safe passage, swift feet, and a journey untroubled by misfortune.

Merchants, too, called upon Hermes, for commerce was travel's twin. Trade bound city to city and shore to shore, its lifeblood flowing through carts, caravans, and ships. As the god who moved freely between realms, Hermes ensured that markets thrived and ventures prospered. His favor was sought not only for protection, but for fortune—for smooth negotiations, profitable exchanges, and the cleverness to see opportunity where others saw risk.

He was not a static deity but one in constant motion—his realm was the space between destinations, the pulse of transactions, the breath of the wandering soul. To walk, to trade, to cross a border—these were acts under Hermes's watchful eye. His essence lived in every threshold, and his blessing turned treacherous roads into sacred journeys.

Hermes's patronage over travelers and merchants reflected his deepest truth: he was the god of passage—between places, between people, between fates. His guidance was not bound to temples or thrones, but wandered the earth with those in motion. Through him, the Greeks honored the spirit of movement, the courage to depart, and the wisdom to navigate the in-between.

God Who Wore a Thousand Faces

Among the many faces of Hermes, none gleamed brighter—or more elusive—than that of the trickster. Where other gods commanded through strength or decree, Hermes moved in shadows, shaping fate through cleverness, laughter, and illusion. His wit was his weapon, his charm a cloak, and his mind a forge where deception became a divine art. To know Hermes was to understand that truth itself could wear many faces—and sometimes, to reveal what matters most, one must first conceal.

His first great act of wit—the theft of Apollo's cattle—set the stage for a god who would forever dance on the edge of order. With infant hands and a mind already sharpened by the divine, Hermes reversed hoofprints, crafted sandals of bark, and wrapped his theft in humor and audacity. He deceived the god of light not with malice, but with brilliance, earning both rebuke and admiration. In every step, he proved that cunning could rival strength—and that mischief, when artful, could bind even the greatest rivals in respect.

But Hermes's trickery extended beyond clever thefts. He was a master of disguise, a shapeshifter who could vanish into any form, slip through barriers unseen, and speak in a thousand voices. In this power lay more than evasion—it was transformation itself. His ability to move between guises symbolized the ever-changing nature of identity, the sacred mutability of spirit, and the power to adapt where others broke.

His mischief, though playful, often carried deeper purpose. In disrupting expectations, Hermes revealed hidden truths. His tricks could unmask hypocrisy, resolve tension, or mend fractured bonds. In every jest, there was intent; in every illusion, a revelation. He was a weaver of riddles whose chaos often restored balance.

Hermes's cunning nature was not a flaw, but a force—a heavenly reminder that not all wisdom wears a solemn face. Through disguise, deception, and delight, he taught that clarity can emerge from confusion, that the unexpected holds special lessons, and that sometimes, the boldest truth comes in the form of a joke well told.

BRIDGE OF REALMS

Hermes stood at the crossroads of mortal and immortal, his presence woven into the rhythm of daily life and the heartbeat of myth. Through speed and eloquence, guidance and guile, he became the god of movement, transition, and connection. Travelers honored him, merchants invoked him, and poets praised the wit behind his ever-shifting form. He transcended boundaries not merely of place, but of identity and purpose—bridging realms with laughter, wisdom, and grace. In Hermes, the Greeks found more than a messenger—they found the spirit of ingenuity itself, ever in motion, ever becoming.

> *"Hermes, the guide of souls,*
> *who through the shadowy paths of the underworld leads*
> *with gentle speech and swift feet, ever the friend of mortals."*
> — *Homer, The Iliad*

Commerce and Exchange

Hermes's influence flowed beyond the realm of myth, coursing through the veins of Greek society as the god of trade and commerce—the deific architect of exchange. In a world where prosperity depended on movement, negotiation, and connection, Hermes was the unseen usher in every transaction, the whisper at every deal, the pulse behind every marketplace.

Merchants called upon him at the outset of every journey, offering prayers and sacrifice before laden carts and sail-filled ships. They sought not only safe passage, but cleverness, fortune, and foresight—the gifts of a god who understood both the risks and rewards of enterprise. Markets and harbors, alive with barter and ambition, were sacred to Hermes, their energy echoing the boundless momentum of his step.

The fluid nature of commerce mirrored Hermes himself— swift, adaptable, and ever between worlds. Just as he moved freely from Olympus to Earth and down into the underworld, so too did trade transcend borders, carrying not only goods but knowledge, language, and culture. Through him, the Greeks saw commerce as more than economic necessity—it was spirited motion, a current of shared destiny.

Hermes's patronage was not blind to the ambiguities of the marketplace. His tales speak of cunning and deception, of profits earned and lines crossed. He was both protector and provocateur, honoring ingenuity while revealing the consequences of overreach. In this balance, he became a symbol not only of gain, but of conscience—reminding mortals that commerce must walk a line between shrewdness and justice.

He championed invention, negotiation, and the art of the deal. But always, Hermes stood at the threshold—not just between buyer and seller, but between wealth and wisdom. His presence reminded mortals that enterprise, when guided by grace and foresight, could uplift cities and unite cultures.

Through trade and commerce, Hermes became the god who linked the material with the meaningful—the divine spark in the clink of coin, the flourish of a contract, the journey of a ship to distant shores. In every act of honest exchange, his spirit stirred: a patron not only of profit, but of purpose.

Emblems of Divine Motion

Two sacred symbols—both elegant and potent—reveal the spirit of Hermes: the caduceus and the winged sandals. These were not mere adornments, but manifestations of the god himself, woven into the myths, temples, and imagination of the ancient world. Through them, Hermes became not just a presence, but a force—of movement, mediation, and meaning.

The caduceus, his famed staff, bore twin serpents spiraling upward in perfect symmetry, crowned with wings. This image held layers of hallowed significance. The serpents, intertwined without conflict, symbolized duality held in harmony—life and death, stillness and motion, truth and illusion. With this staff in hand, Hermes was not only the messenger, but the reconciler—he who calmed strife, brokered peace, and guided souls across thresholds unseen. The caduceus became a symbol of sacred balance, a rod that crossed boundaries yet disturbed none.

It was also a mark of authority and protection. With it, Hermes traversed the realms—Olympus, Earth, and Hades—with sovereign grace. He soothed disputes, whispered counsel, and healed divisions. In later ages, the caduceus would be adopted as a symbol of medicine and diplomacy, but its origin lay in the hands of a god who spoke not only with words, but with wisdom.

Equally iconic were his winged sandals—the Talaria—crafted by Hephaestus and light as air. These divine shoes did not merely grant speed; they made Hermes untethered. He soared across mountains, oceans, and underworld gates, delivering messages, shifting fate, and reweaving the web of myth. In art, they appear delicate yet purposeful—grace fused with intent, speed paired with silence.

Together, the caduceus and the winged sandals form the sacred geometry of Hermes's identity. One grounded in harmony, the other soaring in motion. One to touch the soul, the other to stir the wind. They were more than symbols—they were extensions of the god's essence, echoing his gift for balance, transformation, and the eternal journey between worlds.

God in Verse and Voice

In the pages of Greek literature, Hermes moved with the same grace and subtlety that defined his mythic form—shaping epics, guiding heroes, and leaving behind a trail of wit, wisdom, and wonder. From solemn poetry to comic drama, his presence echoed across genres, his character a mirror for transformation, cleverness, and connection.

In Homer's *Iliad*, Hermes appears not as a warrior, but as a shepherd of dignity and peace. When Priam, king of Troy, dares to enter the Greek camp to ransom his son Hector's body, it is Hermes who escorts him, cloaking the aged king in divine protection. In this moment of stillness amid war, Hermes becomes the quiet force of compassion, the god who guides not only footsteps, but grief.

In the *Odyssey*, his role deepens. When Odysseus faces the enchantress Circe, it is Hermes who delivers salvation—offering the sacred herb moly and the wisdom to withstand her magic. Through this gift, Hermes empowers the mortal hero to resist illusion and reclaim his path. He is not just a guide through space, but through ordeal—a champion of cleverness and resolve.

Outside Homer's epics, Hermes walked the stages of Greek drama. In the comedies of Aristophanes, he takes on a more playful guise—witty, sharp, and irreverently divine. Here, he is the god of laughter and insight, a trickster who lightens tension while revealing truths. His comic portrayal did not diminish his power—it revealed his range. Whether cloaked in solemnity or satire, Hermes brought clarity where confusion reigned.

His literary presence spoke to his universality. As a god of boundaries and transitions, he fit every genre, every theme. He was the whisper in a hero's ear, the shadow between acts, the flash of intelligence that turned crisis into resolution. In stories both sacred and satirical, Hermes stood as a reminder that change is constant—and that with wit and grace, it can be navigated.

Through verse and voice, Hermes endured—a figure of movement, mischief, and meaning. His role in Greek literature was not ornament, but essence: a god whose presence carried stories forward, whose words still echo where journeys begin.

WHISPER BETWEEN WORLDS

Hermes, the winged herald of Olympus, was a god shaped by motion, mind, and mystery. In every myth that bore his name, he moved not just through space, but through meaning—ushering souls into shadow, carrying messages across heaven and earth, and turning the tides of fate with wit and a smile. As trickster, guardian, and guide, Hermes stood at every threshold: between life and death, silence and speech, stillness and journey. His charm was not frivolous—it was sacred. His cleverness not deception, but revelation. He was the god who crossed boundaries and, in doing so, wove them into unity.

His influence, however, extended far beyond Olympus. In the markets of Greece, in the songs of poets, and at the edge of every road, Hermes was present. He watched over commerce and eloquence, travelers and treaties, laughter and transition. The caduceus he bore—serpents entwined in balance, crowned with wings—reflected the harmony he offered in a world of constant change. His sandals, light as thought, carried the will of the gods and the dreams of mortals. In Hermes, the Greeks saw not only a deity, but a force: agile, intelligent, and essential.

Where others ruled, Hermes moved. Where others fought, he persuaded. Where others remained, he passed through—linking gods and mortals, chaos and clarity, loss and return. His presence reminded the Greeks that transformation was sacred, that wit could mend what power could not, and that those who moved between worlds were often the ones who kept them connected.

As we leave behind the laughter and light-footed wisdom of Hermes, we now step into the quiet glow of Hestia. Where Hermes embodies change, Hestia embodies constancy. She is the keeper of flame, the hearth of the home, the still point around which all movement turns. In the next chapter, we explore this often-overlooked goddess—gentle, unshaken, and vital to the heart of Greek life.

CHAPTER 13

HESTIA

Goddess of Hearth and Home

Hestia's myth speaks in quiet tones of devotion, constancy, and mystical stillness—a contrast to the storm of her fellow Olympians. She vowed eternal virginity, forsaking worldly entanglements to become the ever-present guardian of hearth and flame. Her presence was not dramatic, but foundational, offering peace where others sought power. In home and temple alike, she was the sacred flame that bound families and cities in unity. Though she relinquished her Olympian throne, she gained a deeper reverence—her flame not consuming, but sustaining, a divine light that whispered of harmony, belonging, and the timeless sanctuary of home.

> *"Hestia, in the high dwellings of all,*
> *both deathless gods and men who walk on earth,*
> *has an everlasting abode and highest honor."*
> — *Homeric Hymn to Hestia*

Virgin Flame of Olympus

Hestia, firstborn of Cronus and Rhea, stood as a pillar of stillness amid the storm of Olympus. In a realm dominated by passion, power, and divine intrigue, she radiated a quiet majesty—the sacred embodiment of the hearth's eternal flame. As goddess of the home, Hestia represented stability and sanctuary, her influence felt not through thunder or spectacle, but in the steady warmth that anchored both mortal and immortal life. Though her tales are soft-spoken among the clamor of myth, they pulse with enduring reverence.

The turning point in her mythic path came with a solemn vow. Sought by Poseidon, lord of the sea, and Apollo, god of light, Hestia stood unmoved by their pursuit. Her heart, unmarred by longing, desired no union but peace. She turned to Zeus, sovereign of Olympus, and pledged herself to eternal chastity. In honor of her choice, Zeus granted her celestial protection and a seat at the divine hearth, unseen yet ever present.

This vow was no mere renunciation—it was a consecration. In forgoing the entanglements of love and rivalry, Hestia preserved her purpose unclouded. She became the ever-watchful keeper of the flame, tending the eternal light that blazed at the center of every home and every city. Her virginity became a symbol not of absence but of unwavering devotion, an emblem of constancy in a pantheon often swayed by whim and passion.

In choosing solitude over suitors, simplicity over splendor, Hestia distinguished herself from her exalted kin. She sought no throne nor bolt of lightening, no conquest nor chorus of adoration. Yet in her stillness, she held sway over the rhythms of life itself. Her vow sanctified the hearth, made spiritual the domestic, and offered a deific promise that where her flame burned, harmony would reign.

Bearer of the Sacred Flame

At the heart of Hestia's heavenly essence was her Godly guardianship of the hearth—the ever-burning flame that united home, family, and polis in a single thread of sanctity. This fire, more than warmth or sustenance, was the soul of the household, a vessel of continuity passed from generation to generation. As its divine custodian, Hestia stood not in glory or war, but in quiet constancy, embodying harmony, reverence, and the unspoken strength of tradition.

In every Greek home, a fire glowed in her honor—its flickering light a living tribute to the goddess whose presence sanctified daily life. Offerings were cast into the embers before meals, humble tokens of devotion seeking her favor. This same flame that illuminated hearths also burned in the civic centers of city-states, a symbol of shared identity and enduring unity. Where her fire lived, so too did peace and prosperity.

Hestia's role extended into every threshold crossed. When a new home was founded, the first fire was kindled in her name, and when cities rose, her burning embers were planted at their core. Her presence sanctified beginnings, bound communities, and affirmed the sacred bond between mortals and the immortals.

Unlike her fellow Olympians, whose tales roared with conflict and conquest, Hestia's dominion was one of steadiness. Her eternal flame offered not spectacle but sanctuary, not triumph but trust. She was the still center in a world of shifting gods, the ever-burning light that promised order, blessing, and belonging.

Eldest and Most Enduring

Hestia's sacred nature shaped her relationships not through spectacle, but through stillness. While the thrones of Olympus often trembled beneath rivalries, passions, and quarrels, Hestia stood apart—untouched by intrigue, unswayed by ambition. She neither sought dominion nor stirred conflict. Her loyalty remained fixed upon the hearthstone, the sacred flame that bound both mortal and heavenly realms in a covenant of peace.

As the firstborn of Cronus and Rhea, Hestia held a station of deep reverence. Swallowed first by her father and released last through Zeus's revolt, her ordeal became a quiet symbol of patience and inner strength. She bore the silence of centuries without protest, her spirit tempered like iron in burning fire.

Among her kin, Hestia's calm presence became a sanctuary. While gods such as Ares waged battle and Hera plotted vengeance, Hestia nurtured no grudges and demanded no glory. Her impartiality was not weakness—it was wisdom. In her constancy, she commanded respect. She reminded the Olympians that true power lies not in thunder or conquest, but in steadiness—the flame that does not flicker even in the storm.

Her humility reached its most poignant expression when she relinquished her throne on Olympus to Dionysus. No struggle. No lament. She stepped aside with grace, choosing the unbroken circle of the dwelling over the honors of the high seat. And yet, even removed from the court of the Twelve, her influence never waned. The sacred flame burned still in every home and temple, a silent testament to her everlasting role.

Among mortals, Hestia was cherished as a constant presence in daily life. She did not thunder from the heavens or descend in wrath. She dwelled in the quiet warmth of the fire, in the shared meal, the marriage rite, the city's founding spark. Her presence was not proclaimed—it was felt.

Through her sacred vow, her guardianship of the hearth, and her gentle sovereignty among the gods, Hestia became the embodiment of peace, fidelity, and enduring light. She asked for nothing, yet gave everything—a goddess whose strength lay in stillness, whose divinity burned not in battle, but in the quiet flame that never dies.

FLAME OF PEACE AND UNITY

Hestia's radiant power resided not in conquest, but in constancy. As protector of the lodging, she bestowed peace upon the home and sanctity upon the flame. Her presence blessed every meal, every gathering, every ritual of welcome. She upheld the hallowed duty of hospitality, where guest and host met under her watchful gaze. In cities, her embers burned as a symbol of unity, linking household and polis in shared devotion. Through stillness and light, Hestia wove together the strands of domestic and civic life, embodying the enduring strength of harmony, fidelity, and sacred tradition.

> *"Hestia, who in the high halls of the immortal gods has the chiefest place, and receives the richest portion."*
> — *Hesiod, Theogony*

Guardian of Hearth and Harmony

Hestia's power as goddess of the home was born not of spectacle, but of mythic constancy. She reigned as the deific protector of domestic life, her presence flickering in every fire that warmed the residences of ancient Greece. The hearth she claimed was no mere stone enclosure—it was the soul of the household, a sacred altar where warmth met spirit, where the invisible bonds of kinship were kept aglow by her eternal flame.

Her guardianship touched every corner of daily life. At the hearth, meals were prepared with reverence, stories passed from elder to child, and prayers lifted on tendrils of smoke. Each gathering began and ended in her honor, with the first morsel of food and sip of drink offered in quiet devotion. In these acts, the Greeks reaffirmed their gratitude for her unseen yet ever-present grace, trusting that her favor would preserve the harmony within their walls.

Yet Hestia's flame kindled more than fire—it sustained peace. Where discord threatened to darken the threshold, her calming presence offered renewal. She was invoked in times of quarrel as a spirit of reconciliation, a gentle force restoring balance within the family. In a world where the home was not only shelter but also the heart of civic life, her protection was both sacred and essential.

Unlike her fellow Olympians, whose spheres were marked by conquest or bedlam, Hestia's influence was quiet, omnipresent, and universal. She belonged to no one alone, yet to everyone alike. From palace to humble cottage, her flame burned equally bright, bestowing stability, sanctity, and peace. As the guardian of hearth and harmony, Hestia endured not through triumph, but through the gentle, eternal radiance of devotion.

Patroness of Hospitality

Hospitality—xenia—stood not as mere custom, but as sacred law in the hearts of the ancient Greeks, and at its center burned the gentle flame of Hestia. As patroness of the hearth and holy host of all homes, her celestial presence sanctified the act of welcoming stranger and kin alike. In extending bread, warmth, and shelter, mortals honored not only one another, but the goddess who presided silently over every threshold.

The hearthstone, ever tended in her name, was often the first sight upon entering a dwelling—a beacon of refuge and goodwill.

To light a fire for a guest was to invoke Hestia herself, and in that glow, the weary found peace. Her invisible hand guided hosts in the rituals of reception, ensuring their offerings were more than gestures—they were sacred oaths of respect, comfort, and trust. To violate this trust was to defy the divine, for neglect of xenia was an affront not only to guest, but to goddess.

Hestia's grace extended beyond private halls to great feasts and public gatherings. She was the first to be honored in offerings, her flame lit before food was served or hymns sung. In her name, harmony reigned over the table, and celebration took on a solemn beauty. Through her, hospitality was lifted from obligation to blessing—an act through which both host and guest became partakers in the sacred.

Yet perhaps her noblest charge lay with the unknown traveler. In a land where roads were treacherous and faces unfamiliar, Hestia whispered to mortals a timeless truth: that kindness to the stranger is kindness to the gods. Hers was a welcome that knew no walls, a warmth that reached beyond hearthstone and city gate. In every act of hospitality, her eternal fire endured.

Flame of the Polis

Hestia's sacred fire did not flicker solely within the walls of the home—it blazed at the heart of the city. As guardian of the public hearth, she was the divine thread that wove domestic sanctity into civic unity. In every polis of ancient Greece, her flame burned ceaselessly in temples and town centers, tended with reverence as a symbol of enduring order and shared identity. To let it die was to court dissolution; to keep it burning was to affirm the life of the community itself.

At the founding of a new colony, fire was drawn from the mother city's central hearth and carried with solemn ceremony across land and sea. That sacred spark, born of Hestia, ignited the first flame in a new land—a bond between old and new, past and future. Her fire did not merely warm the body; it sustained the soul of civilization, marking continuity of lineage, tradition, and purpose.

During public rites and festivals, Hestia's presence was always first and last—honored with offerings before gods of war or revelry, as though to affirm that from her peace all things rightfully began. Her blessings were invoked to sanctify the gathering, inviting concord to dwell where crowds might clash. In honoring Hestia, the people called upon the spirit of kinship and sacred duty.

Yet her influence reached beyond altars and assemblies. In the values she inspired—generosity, moderation, respect—Hestia shaped the very spirit of public life. She reminded mortals that a community, like a home, must be tended, and that harmony among citizens was as vital as flame to fire.

Through hearth and ritual, through home and city, Hestia's flame bound all together. Silent but eternal, hers was the light that steadied the world.

AT THE HEART OF ALL THINGS

Hestia's presence imbued Greek life with sacred cohesion—her eternal flame burned at the heart of both home and polis, binding the realms of mortal and divine. In temples and households alike, her fire sanctified the rhythms of daily life and the rituals of shared tradition. Celebrated through solemn festivals and quiet offerings, she embodied the spirit of peace, duty, and celestial belonging. As the ever-steady defender of the hearth, Hestia stood as a symbol of unity, her unseen grace weaving stability and harmony through the fabric of Greek culture.

> *"Hestia, you who tend the sacred hearth of the immortal gods, ever the honored and eternal flame at the heart of every home."*
> — *Homeric Hymn to Hestia*

Hearthfire of Home and Temple

In the sacred rhythm of Greek life, the hearth was no mere hearthstone—it was a consecrated flame, the beating heart of both home and polis. Wherever a fire glowed—be it in humble kitchens or great city temples—it burned in honor of Hestia, the goddess of warmth, unity, and unbroken presence. To her belonged the fire that linked the mortal to the immortal, the domestic to the civic, the individual to the whole.

Within private homes, the hearth was more than a source of heat; it was a living altar. Here, families gathered to cook, commune, and offer prayers. Each meal began and ended with tribute to Hestia, as a token of gratitude and devotion. A libation spilled into the flames, a whispered invocation—these rituals ensured her blessings lingered in the very air, sanctifying daily life with divine constancy.

Beyond the threshold of the home, her flame blazed in the prytaneia, the civic hearths of towns and temples. These divine fires, kept perpetually lit, embodied the strength and spirit of the community. They were kindled from the ancestral fire of the mother city, forging bonds across generations and settlements. To extinguish one was a dire omen; to light one anew, a rite of rebirth and collective hope.

As guardian of the eternal flame, Hestia bridged solitude and society. Her quiet dominion united homes and cities under a single sacred fire, a reminder that the essence of peace begins not with power, but with presence, warmth, and shared reverence.

Rites of Flame and Fellowship

Though Hestia's presence was a daily sanctity—woven into the breath of hearth fires and whispered prayers—she was also honored through solemn festivals and sacred rites that echoed her quiet majesty. Unlike the resounding processions and theatrical spectacles devoted to other Olympians, the celebrations of Hestia were serene, steeped in reverence rather than revelry, and grounded in the virtues she embodied: unity, constancy, and devotion.

Among these observances was the Hestiaia, a festival held in various city-states, where citizens gathered around lodgings both public and private to offer libations, bread, and shared meals. These humble acts reflected the goddess's nature—unassuming yet essential, invisible yet ever present—reminding all who partook of the spiritual flame that burned within each home and heart.

Her sacred presence also graced greater festivals, such as the Panathenaic rites in Athens, where Hestia's blessings were invoked to sanctify the city's spirit and ensure communal peace. In the founding of distant colonies, it was Hestia's fire—carried from the mother city—that kindled the first hearth of the new land, a ritual of continuity that consecrated the bond between old and new.

These rituals, though modest, carried immense symbolic power. They did not seek spectacle, but sanctity. In each shared meal, each carefully lit fire, the Greeks reaffirmed their connection to Hestia—the eternal flame that warmed their homes, united their cities, and kindled their souls.

Ember of the Eternal Flame

Hestia's legacy burned quietly but unceasingly within the soul of Greek households. Unlike the thunderous myths of war and passion, hers was a sacred constancy—woven into the rhythms of daily life, felt in the warmth of a meal, the light of a fire, and the silence of shared peace. She was not merely honored in temples or invoked at festivals—she was lived, her mythic presence rekindled each time the hearth flame was tended with care.

Among the most enduring traditions was the ritual lighting of a new household fire. When two souls joined in marriage and crossed the threshold of their home, they would kindle a flame dedicated to Hestia. This act marked not just the beginning of domestic life, but the welcome of the goddess herself into the heart of the home. That fire, once lit, was nurtured daily—its glow a pledge of harmony, fidelity, and divine guardianship.

Yet Hestia's reach extended beyond the flickering embers. She presided over the values the hearth embodied: peace, unity, and continuity. Her unseen hand calmed disputes, softened grief, and hallowed the joys of kinship. As the spiritual anchor of the household, Hestia reminded mortals that the truest sanctuaries were not always built of stone, but of love, constancy, and shared devotion.

Though centuries passed and cities rose and fell, the reverence for Hestia endured. She remained a symbol of enduring grace, her burning embers linking the ancient past to each present moment, wherever warmth, welcome, and unity lived.

FLAME AT THE WORLD'S CENTER

Among the storm-swept heights of Olympus, Hestia remained ever still—her eternal light undimmed, her purpose unwavering. While her immortal kin thundered across myth and legend with tales of war, passion, and intrigue, she tended the sacred hearth, quietly binding the cosmos with warmth, order, and unity. As guardian of both household and polis, Hestia's presence was less a tale than a truth—eternal, comforting, and essential.

Her hallowed embers glowed in every Greek home and temple, not as spectacle, but as a living symbol of continuity. In her, the Greeks found serenity amid strife, constancy amid anarchy. She did not seek glory or conquest, but chose devotion. Her decision to yield her place among the Twelve Olympians to Dionysus was not an act of retreat, but of wisdom—an embodiment of humility and peace over pride and power.

While the other Olympians roared with power and passion, Hestia's legacy endured in silence—in the flicker of peaceful hearthfires, in the bond of family, in every flame kindled in peace. From the quiet glow of the domestic hearth to the great civic fires that pulsed with communal life, her influence shaped the moral architecture of ancient Greece. Hospitality, fidelity, and sacred duty—these were the values she nurtured and kept alive. Her myth was not shouted—it was whispered, lived, and passed through generations in the simple, mythic act of tending the flame.

Now, as we step away from the steady warmth of her flame, we enter a realm where fire dances rather than glows—a world of frenzy, ecstasy, and radiant liberation. In the next chapter, we follow Dionysus, god of wine and madness, into the wild heart of celebration and transformation, where joy and chaos entwine, and life renews itself in sacred revelry.

CHAPTER 14

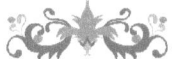

DIONYSUS

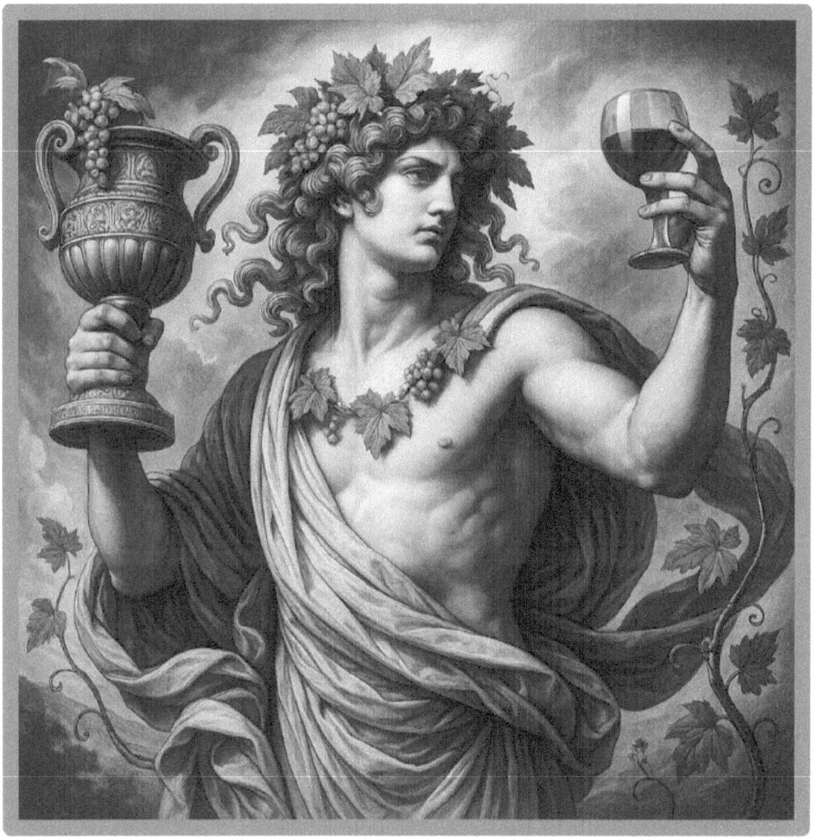

God of Wine and Celebration

Dionysus, god of wine, ecstasy, and transformation, holds a singular place among the Olympians. Born of divine fire and mortal fragility, his tale is one of resilience and revelation. From his miraculous birth to his wandering across distant lands, he spread the heavenly art of winemaking and the liberation of the soul. Rejected by kings and embraced by outcasts, Dionysus triumphed not through force, but through joy, delirium, and supernatural rapture. His myth stands as a testament to the power of rebirth and the eternal dance between suffering and transcendence.

> *"And the god of the grapevine,*
> *Dionysus, gave men the joy of wine*
> *and the madness that falls upon*
> *those who drink too deeply."*
> — *Euripides, The Bacchae*

Twice-Born God

The birth of Dionysus unfolds as one of the most wondrous and perilous tales in the mythic tapestry of Greece. Born of the union between Zeus, sovereign of the heavens, and Semele, a mortal princess of Thebes, his origin bridged the eternal and the ephemeral. Yet the promise of life was shadowed by exalted rage. When Hera, queen of the gods, discovered Zeus's affair, her fury knew no bounds. Cloaked in deception, she took the form of a trusted handmaiden and planted a fatal seed of doubt in Semele's heart.

Urged by Hera's cunning, Semele demanded that Zeus reveal himself in his true divine form. Bound by an unbreakable oath, the thunderer unveiled his godhood in a blaze of celestial fire. No mortal could withstand such radiance. Semele was consumed in the transcendent conflagration, leaving only ashes behind. But from that ruin, life clung to hope. Zeus, in a final act of love, gathered the unborn child and stitched him into his own thigh, sheltering the god-to-be within the flesh of Olympus.

From this strange womb, Dionysus was born again—twice-born, hallowed and undying. This miraculous rebirth became the emblem of his essence: life emerging from destruction, joy rising from sorrow. After his second birth, Hermes bore the infant to the hidden vale of Nysa, where gentle nymphs cradled him in secret and sang lullabies beneath the shade of sacred trees.

There, in the quiet hush of the wild, Dionysus learned the mysteries of the vine. He coaxed sweetness from the grape and brought forth the art of winemaking—his gift to gods and mortals alike. His earliest steps echoed the rhythms of rebirth and revelation, the first notes of a heavenly song that would soon intoxicate the world.

Wine, Wildness, and Revelation

Dionysus was no god of stillness or silence. Restless as the wind through vineyard leaves, he roamed across Greece and beyond—to the temples of Egypt, the mountains of Phrygia, the far reaches of India. Wherever his foot touched earth, he carried with him the secret of the vine, and with it, the promise of joy, release, and reckless abandonment. His procession shimmered with wildness—satyrs danced, nymphs sang, and the frenzied maenads cried out in rapture, their movements echoing the primal heartbeat of nature.

But these were not idle travels. They were Godly journeys of transformation. Dionysus brought not only wine, but the upheaval and renewal that followed in its wake. His path was one of liberation—of cities awakened, minds unshackled, and truths revealed beneath the veil of elation. To those who welcomed him, he brought blessings. To those who mocked him, he became the god of retribution. When foolish sailors tried to seize him, he wrapped their ship in vines and turned them into dolphins, casting them into the sea in a flash of exalted fury.

Among kings and mortals, his miracles taught deeper truths. He granted Midas the power of gold, only for it to become a curse—a bitter lesson about the emptiness of greed. Yet his gifts were not merely warnings. Through wine and ritual, Dionysus revealed a rapturous release, a sacred possession that could lift the soul beyond the confines of reason. In his wake, the world danced, wept, and awakened to something ancient and eternal—a jubilation that transcended the mundane and touched the gods.

From Madness to Olympus

Dionysus's path to Olympus was carved through trials and defiance. Among the fiercest of these came in Thebes, the city of his mortal birth. There, King Pentheus mocked his divinity and sought to crush the wild freedom of his rites. But Dionysus, veiled in mortal guise, allowed himself to be seized—not as a victim, but as a god weaving justice through illusion. He unleashed untamed delirium upon the women of Thebes, drawing them to Mount Cithaeron in ecstatic abandon. Among them was Pentheus's own mother, Agave. Blinded by frenzy, she mistook her son for a beast and, with the others, tore him limb from limb.

This tale, immortalized in Euripides' *The Bacchae*, is no mere warning—it is a revelation. To deny Dionysus is to deny transformation, joy, and the sacred chaos that liberates the soul. His vengeance was not born of cruelty, but of necessity: a god's answer to mortal hubris.

Yet from wrath rose vindication. In time, the gods welcomed him to Olympus, not as a usurper, but as one of their own. His ascent signified more than personal triumph—it was the heavenly embrace of outsiders, of ecstasy, of renewal. Dionysus became a champion of those who danced at the edges of the world, a god whose laughter shook the walls of convention. His spirit infused the theater, where masks fell and truth emerged through performance. Through Dionysus, the veil between illusion and revelation grew thin—and mortals, if only briefly, tasted the divine madness that frees and transforms.

EUPHORIA AND TRANSFORMATION

Dionysus, lord of the vine and bearer of Godly delight, wielded powers that reached into the soul of humanity. His dominion was not confined to wine and revelry—it embraced the mysteries of transformation, the unraveling of order, and the rapture of rebirth. He stirred madness and joy in equal measure, dissolving boundaries between mortal and immortal. Through intoxication and ritual, he unveiled hidden truths, granting vision through abandon. In Dionysus lived the eternal rhythm of nature—growth, decay, and renewal—offering a glimpse into life's feral, sacred pulse, where pleasure met revelation and mayhem danced with clarity.

*"Under the influence of Dionysus,
the bounds of the ordinary break,
and the soul finds wings to soar
beyond the everyday world."*
— *Orphic Hymns*

Wine, Rapture, and Unshackled Soul

Dionysus, the embodied alchemist of joy, gifted mortals the mystical mystery of the vine. More than a god of wine, he was a liberator of the soul, dissolving the rigid forms of daily life through the ecstatic power of his gifts. Wine, under his celestial influence, was not mere indulgence—it was transformation. In the *Homeric Hymn*, he is praised as "the giver of joy," whose nectar brings delight, unshackles the heart, and opens the door to the immortal.

Dionysus taught humanity how to cultivate grapes and unlock the spirit hidden within the fruit. To drink in his name was to enter communion with something beyond mortal bounds. The act was sacred—a ritual that bridged earth and Olympus, flesh and spirit. But his power did not end with the cup. Dionysus ruled over frenzy, ecstasy, and unbound mania. His presence awakened what lay buried: passion, truth, sorrow, and wild delight.

In the Dionysia—festivals held in his honor—the veil of civilization was briefly lifted. Processions wound through cities, choruses sang, and actors donned masks to perform tragedies and comedies alike. These rites, both theatrical and heavenly, were not distractions but revelations. They celebrated the primal, the instinctual, the parts of human nature that society often concealed.

His followers, the maenads and satyrs, embodied this ecstatic liberation. Their dance was a prayer, their revelry a ritual. In Dionysus's world, joy was sacred, hysteria divine, and through him, mortals could glimpse the unbound rhythms of life and death.

Madness and Metamorphosis

Among the most potent of Dionysus's special gifts was his power to transform—not only the forms of men and beasts, but the very boundaries of perception and reason. In myth, he turned a crew of lawless sailors into dolphins, their laughter drowned in salt and song, a warning to those who dared defy the god of liberation. Yet such outward transmutations were only echoes of the deeper transformations he wielded: the unraveling of minds, the reshaping of souls.

Dionysus did not impose delirium merely to punish, but to awaken. His transcendent frenzy could fracture the barriers of the self, exposing hidden truths buried beneath the façade of order. For those who mocked his divinity, like King Lycurgus, the descent into lunacy was swift and ruinous—visions and illusions replacing reason until only destruction remained. But for those who embraced the god, madness became a sacred path.

Through the Dionysian Mysteries, initiates surrendered to ecstatic rites that dissolved their mortal limits. In this primordial unrest, they found rebirth. The veil of illusion lifted, and they emerged transformed—touched by a divine awareness that bridged the realms of man and god. Dionysus, ever the liminal deity, danced at the edge of reason and rapture, reminding mortals that truth sometimes lies not in clarity, but in the beautiful disarray of rapturous trance.

Wine, Grave, and Flame

Dionysus, the twice-born god, stood as an Olympian emblem of the eternal cycle—life, death, and resurrection flowing in seamless rhythm. His own mythic origin reflected this mystic truth. Born of mortal Semele and fathered by Zeus, Dionysus was rescued from his mother's fiery demise and reborn from the god's immortal thigh. This miraculous second birth marked him not just as a deity of joy, but as a symbol of renewal—proof that life may rise anew from ruin.

This theme echoed through the natural world he governed. In the vineyard, where the vine withers in winter and revives with spring, Dionysus's spirit pulsed with every bud and harvest. He was not merely a god of intoxication, but of transformation—of endings that became beginnings, of mortality pierced by divine resurgence.

In his rites and mysteries, initiates enacted symbolic deaths to be reborn in spirit. The shedding of worldly burdens, of reason and restraint, allowed worshippers to touch the sacred current of regeneration. To follow Dionysus was to abandon the known and be remade—purified through exultation, renewed through surrender.

More than a reveler, Dionysus was a god of profound insight. He revealed that beneath the chaos of life and the silence of death lies an ancient rhythm. Those who dared drink from his chalice, who danced in his exalted frenzy, might find not only delight, but immortality of spirit—reborn in the wine, the earth, and the myth that endures.

ECHOES OF THE LIBERATOR

Dionysus, god of wine, joy, and spiritual release, left an indelible imprint upon Greek culture. His spirit surged through the great festivals of Dionysia, where drama and ritual blurred the line between mortal and immortal. In theater, art, and celestial revelry, he became a patron of creative freedom and emotional truth. More than a bringer of joy, Dionysus was a liberator of the soul—one who shattered constraint and awakened wonder. His legacy endures wherever celebration becomes a way of life and the human spirit dares to dance beyond its bounds.

> *"In holy Thebes, where the vine blooms*
> *and the joy of Dionysus fills the hearts of men,*
> *the god of ecstasy is honored with dance and song."*
> *— Euripides, The Bacchae*

Sacred Stage of Dionysia

Among the great celebrations of ancient Greece, none echoed the spirit of Dionysus more vividly than the Festival of Dionysia. Held each spring in Athens, this grand rite honored the god of wine, ecstasy, and theatre—a convergence of heavenly ritual and cultural spectacle. Citizens gathered from across the Greek world, drawn by the promise of revelry, dramatic art, and communion with the divine.

The festival unfolded in stages: processions bearing sacred symbols, offerings to Dionysus, and days of feasting and festivity.

At its heart stood the theatre—an altar of storytelling where human emotion and divine mystery met. Tragedies and comedies written by masters like Aeschylus, Sophocles, and Euripides were performed not as mere entertainment, but as special offerings. Through these dramas, audiences confronted the forces of fate, hubris, love, and vengeance, guided always by the presence of Dionysus—the god who broke boundaries and awakened truth through rapture.

During the Dionysia, the ordinary was overturned. Masks concealed faces, but revealed deeper selves. Wine flowed, dissolving barriers between citizen and stranger, ruler and servant. It was a time of spiritual license, where joy was holy, and sorrow could be sanctified through art.

The Festival of Dionysia stood as more than a celebration. It was a gateway—a moment when mortals stepped beyond themselves and, through ritual and performance, glimpsed the eternal. In the theatre of Dionysus, myth was made flesh, and the soul was stirred by the eternal fire of transformation.

God Behind the Mask

Dionysus's spirit danced through the heart of ancient drama, shaping Greek theatre into a sacred vessel for divine expression. As the patron god of the stage, he was more than muse—he was presence. Theatres bearing his name rose across Greece, the most renowned being the great Theatre of Dionysus in Athens, carved into the slopes of the Acropolis and capable of holding thousands. These were not mere halls of performance—they were sanctuaries, where myth was given voice and the human soul was laid bare.

In his honor, playwrights composed tragedies and comedies that plumbed the depths of mortal and immortal struggle. Tragedies unspooled the threads of destiny and downfall, while comedies gave voice to satire, folly, and redemption. The stage became a mirror of Dionysus himself—ecstatic and destructive, joyful and mad—offering spectators both catharsis and communion.

His essence infused every mask, every chorus, every rising lament and thunderous laughter. Through the power of dramatic ritual, the audience did not merely watch—they transformed. Boundaries dissolved. Emotion was exorcised. And in that sacred space between light and shadow, Dionysus offered revelation.

To the Greeks, theatre was not a diversion but a rite. It was a gift of Dionysus, who taught that through story, mortals could confront the mysteries of existence, taste the wine of truth, and emerge changed. In every cry upon the stage, his voice echoed; in every silent tear, his craziness and mercy lingered.

ECSTASY OF IMMORTALITY

Dionysus stands among the Olympians as a radiant paradox—god of wine and primordial release, but also of transformation, revelation, and rebirth. His presence was not confined to the vineyard or the theatre; it coursed through the spirit of Greek society as a force of spiritual liberation. Where the world imposed order, Dionysus dissolved boundaries. Through his rites and mysteries, he welcomed all who dwelled at the margins—women, foreigners, the mad, the misunderstood—and offered them freedom not just of body, but of soul. His cult became a sanctuary for self-discovery, equality, and the ecstatic dissolution of social constraint.

In every goblet of wine and each untamed dance, Dionysus revealed the dual nature of existence: joy and sorrow, order and chaos, life and death intertwined. His essence echoed through the theatre, where mortals played out the truths of their condition, and through philosophy, where minds like Nietzsche's saw in him the pulse of life unbound. The Dionysian spirit—unbound, primal, divine—became a symbol of the human need to transcend, to feel deeply, and to live freely.

Dionysus's tale is one of triumph over denial, of joy claimed through pain, and of the revelation found in ecstasy. He invites us to embrace life in its fullness—wild, beautiful, terrifying, and true. As the last of the Olympians to ascend, he reminds us that the gods are not only rulers of nature, but reflections of the soul. And in Dionysus, that soul dances, weeps, and rises again.

Now, as the celestial tales of each Olympian draw to a close, we turn to the legacy they leave behind. The myths, powers, and cultural echoes of the gods are more than ancient stories—they are eternal truths that shaped a civilization and continue to stir the imagination of the modern world.

EPILOGUE

ECHOES OF
OLYMPUS

Ancient Greece

Before ink touched parchment and verse found scroll, the tales of the Olympians were carried by breath and memory—passed from elder to youth, from oracle to poet, from firelit feast to solemn temple. These stories, born of wonder and shaped by awe, gave form to gods and meaning to mystery. They endure not as relics of the past, but as sacred mirrors—reflecting the questions, longings, and truths that define the human spirit.

At the summit of these divine legends rose Mount Olympus, the mythic seat of celestial power. Cloaked in cloud and crowned with stars, it was not merely the home of the gods but the threshold between the mortal and the eternal. Here, Zeus thundered judgment, Athena wove strategy, and Dionysus danced between joy and madness. Yet Olympus, for all its grandeur, was never perfect. Its gods were glorious and flawed, mighty and vulnerable—echoes of ourselves carved in mythic likeness.

Greek mythology stands as a cornerstone of Western imagination and a bridge between cultures. Its myths are not isolated tales, but vital threads in the shared tapestry of global storytelling—intertwining with Roman, Norse, Egyptian, and Vedic traditions. Across continents and centuries, the gods speak through art, literature, and memory, challenging us to ponder fate, justice, beauty, and the burden of choice.

This book is your passage into that mythic realm—a journey across radiant peaks and shadowed valleys, where thunderbolts shape destinies and whispers of prophecy guide the soul. Through gods and monsters, vengeance and love, triumph and tragedy, you have walked beside immortals and glimpsed the eternal dance between chaos and order.

As the final pages turn, the myths do not end—they awaken. The Olympians, ageless in their splendor and strife, continue to live on in every story retold, every truth sought, every dream dared. May their voices echo through your thoughts, may their struggles inspire your own ascent, and may the path you now walk be lit by the wisdom and wonder of the old gods.

> "*Sing now, O Muse, of the gods who dwell on Olympus high...*"
> —*Homeric Hymn*

ABOUT THE
AUTHOR

Seeker of Stories, Weaver of Myth

Michael J. Defosse is a published author with a background in the business world and a passion for storytelling. He holds an undergraduate degree in Economics and two graduate degrees from Syracuse University, bringing a unique blend of analytical thinking and creative inspiration to his work. His previous books, primarily focused on finance and risk management, showcased his expertise in his professional field. However, his love for mythology, folklore, and fantasy has guided him toward a new literary adventure.

Growing up in a small town surrounded by nature, Michael spent his childhood exploring the forest behind his home and fishing in the nearby lake. These early experiences fostered a deep connection with the natural world, allowing his imagination to wander through the myths and legends of ancient cultures. The quiet of the woods and the mysteries of the lake often brought to mind the stories of gods, heroes, and mythical creatures that would later inspire his writing.

With his new five-book series on Greek mythology, Michael combines his lifelong love of mythology with his talent for storytelling. Each book in the series invites readers to explore the ancient world, bringing the timeless tales of the Greek gods and their adventures to life. Michael hopes his stories will ignite the imaginations of readers of all ages, much as his own imagination was sparked by his childhood walks in the forest.

NEXT IN THE SERIES

Greek Mythology: Kingdom of Hades

Underworld Myths, Chthonic Gods, and the Secrets of the Dead

Descend into the veiled dominion beneath the earth—where silence reigns, souls are judged, and gods of shadow hold eternal court.

In this haunting and mythic second volume of the *Greek Mythology* series by Michael J Defosse, explore the sacred architecture of the ancient Underworld. Meet Hades, the silent sovereign of the dead, who governs with unyielding law. Witness Persephone's descent and divine transformation from maiden to Queen of Shadows. Walk the blackened banks of the River Styx. Discover the five rivers, the gates, the judges, and the realms where mortal fate is forever sealed.

Encounter spectral guardians, fallen heroes, and timeless oaths sworn upon waters no god dares betray. This is not a land of torment, but of consequence—where every soul is weighed, and every passage carries meaning.

Through cinematic storytelling and ancient verse, this journey reveals a world not of fear —but of reckoning, reflection, and the threshold to the eternal.

Where death is not the end—but the beginning of truth.

Available soon on Amazon and wherever books from Mythology Publishing are sold.

Continue the Journey

www.MythologyPublishing.com

Thank You for Joining Me on This Journey!

We hope you enjoyed *Greek Mythology: Gods of Mount Olympus* and found it both interesting and insightful. Your thoughts matter to us, and your book review can make a significant difference by helping other readers discover this book.

Share Your Thoughts!

If you enjoyed this book, please consider leaving a review on Amazon or your favorite book review site. Your feedback will not only guide future readers but also support me in creating even better content for upcoming publications.

How to Leave a Review on Amazon:

1. **Visit the Book Page:**
   Go to the *Greek Mythology: Gods of Mount Olympus* product page on Amazon.

2. **Sign In:**
   Make sure you're logged into your Amazon account.

3. **Share Your Thoughts:**
   o Scroll down to the **Customer Reviews** section.

   o Click the **Write a Customer Review** button.

   o Share what you loved about the book—whether it was the stories, the mythology, or the characters.

Your Opinion Matters!

Your honest review not only helps other readers but also enables me to continue bringing the fascinating world of mythology to life.

Stay in Touch!

I'd love to hear more from you. If you have additional comments or thoughts, feel free to reach out directly at **info@mythologypublishing.com**.

Thank you for being part of this mythological journey!

Sincerely,
Michael J. Defosse

www.ingramcontent.com/pod-product-compliance
Lightning Source LLC
Chambersburg PA
CBHW031459120626
46545CB00005B/1678